Boaties' Tales

Amazing stories from New Zealand and the world of boating

Peter Jessup

First published in 2011 by Hurricane Press Ltd
PO Box 568, Cambridge 3450, New Zealand
www.hurricane-press.co.nz

Copyright © 2011 Peter Jessup

Cover image: TRANZ / Corbis
Anchor illustration © Openko Dmytro | Dreamstime.com

National Library of New Zealand Cataloguing-in-Publication Data

Jessup, Peter, 1958–
Boaties' tales : incredible stories from New Zealand and the world
of boating / by Peter Jessup.
ISBN 978-0-9864684-1-4
1. Boats and boating—New Zealand. 2 Boats and boating. I. Title.
797.10993—dc 22

Printed by Bookbuilders, China.

*H*urricane *Press*
books that blow you away

Contents

Foreword

'It isn't that life ashore is distasteful to me, but life at sea is better.'
— Sir Francis Drake, English naval captain (1540–1596).

Water covers about 70% of the earth's surface, and all but 3% of it is salt water. It's no wonder, therefore, that man has been fascinated by the sea, and where it takes him, since the first tree trunk was hollowed out and set afloat.

Forget the wheel — whoever invented the sail was responsible for man's obsession with exploration. And so much more . . .

We've been mucking about in boats for ever. We've used them for food. We've used them for war. We've used them for fun.

But why do some boats sink? Why do some people

survive shipwrecks while others perish around them? And why can't some people just remember to put the bung in before they launch off the local boat ramp?

There are lessons in disaster, big and small, and history provides many answers.

My career as a journalist has enabled me to sail with the navy, and I've worked on commercial fishing boats, crewed on racing yachts and been an avid small boat angler for more than forty years.

With this collection of nautical stories, I've tried to provide some entertainment, as well as enlightenment, for those who love the smell of the sea and a love of the ocean.

— Peter Jessup

Superstitions

'*Mackerel skies and mare's tails, soon will be time to shorten sails.*'
'*Red sky at night, sailor's delight*
Red sky in the morning, sailor's warning.'
— *Old seafarers' proverbs.*

Sailors are a superstitious bunch, and prayers and sacrifices to various Gods of the Sea play a large part in maritime history.

The traditions start with the Greeks and their god, Poseidon, said to be the brother of Zeus and Hades, who was depicted as bearded, bare–chested and carrying a trident. The Etruscan word for Poseidon was 'Nehtun' and from this, the Romans adapted the name to Neptune, who was brother of Jupiter and Pluto.

He was shown in the same form as Poseidon in Roman art and sculpture.

In both mythologies, the God of the Sea was said to be able to keep the waters calm or, if angered, to throw up storms and cause shipwrecks, or to becalm ships until sailors died of hunger and thirst.

And so sacrifices were offered up for safe passage. Alexander the Great is said to have slaughtered four horses and thrown them, and the chariot they had pulled, into the sea, before crossing to Syria to engage in the Battle of Issus.

More recently, mock homage was paid to Neptune when sailing ships crossed the equator. Those who had made the trip before performed a ritual of dressing up as Neptune and his first mate, Davy Jones. They then harangued first–timers, known as 'Pollywogs,' who graduated to be 'Shellbacks' after the ceremony and completing the trip.

Polynesians have their God of the Sea too and there is a remarkable similarity in the way Pacific Island groups pronounce and spell his name.

The Maori have Tangaroa, son of Ranginui, the Sky, and Papatuanuku, Earth.

The first fish caught by a Maori is always put back as an offering to Tangaroa.

This is the name also used by Cook Islanders. In Samoa and Tonga, it is Tagaloa. The Solomon Islanders call him Tangagoa. In the Marquesas, it is Tana'oa.

Superstitions

THE CHRISTENING and naming of a boat are ancient traditions steeped in seafaring superstition.

In Babylonian times, new boats were launched with a religious ceremony and the slaughter of goats as offering to the Gods of the Sea, with the boat then doused in wine for good luck. This type of practice spread through the Greek and then Roman empires; thus it travelled through Europe and then the rest of the world.

And so we have the tradition of breaking a bottle of Champagne on the bow of new ships.

The reason a woman performs this rite is that in the old days, seafarers were 'married to the sea'.

And so comes another tradition — that of captains naming their vessels for the woman they love.

Through early civilisation, boats always had female names. Even as that tradition has fallen away, skippers continue to refer to their craft as 'she'. It demonstrates a captain's love for his ship.

One boat–naming superstition suggests it's unlucky to rename a previously–owned boat. Some say it is bad luck if you remove an old name on a vessel.

Legend has it you can christen the boat with a new name, provided all traces of the previous name are erased, including on ownership papers, and items such as key rings are sent to Davy Jones' Locker.

Once that is done, splash some Champagne across the bow, offer some prayers to the Gods of the Sea and you'll have nothing to worry about. Or so they say.

≈ ≈ ≈

OWNERS TAKE PRIDE in coming up with quirky and amusing names for their boats. Often these have a story behind them.

Here's one: 'When we first towed our first boat, the trailer became unhitched on a downhill slope and the kids in the back of the van started screaming, "Look, the boat is passing us!" Since then, the boat has been called *Run Away*.

In Wanaka, hubby bought a new jet boat. His wife was heard in the background a few times, commenting 'that's my new kitchen' a reference to the boat being bought instead of an upgrade to their house. Shortly after, the boat was named . . . *My New Kitchen*.

Sometimes, you have to wonder what the reactions will be if particular boats get into trouble and have to make a radio call for coastguard assistance.

I've seen boats called *Far Canal* and *Master Baiter*. Also on the saucy theme, there's a yacht named *Blue Vein Throbber*, another labelled *Blow Me* and there is also a *Wet Dream*, and one called *Floating Seamen*.

And a catamaran named *Double Penetration*. Or if inland you could go for *Sir Osis of the River*.

Fishermen like to make the play on being off work, as in *Bin Workin'*, *The Office*, *Dayz Off* or *Off The Hook*. They also like plays on fishing terms as in *Reel Time* or *Reel Determined*, *Reelefishent*, *Big Bites* and *Cod Squad*. There are Kiwi offshore game boats called *Pursuit*, *Outer Limits*, *Hookin' Bull* and *Reel Passion*.

For yachts: *Makin' Luff*, *Blown Aweigh*, *Sails Office* and *Sails Manager*, and for the flamboyantly flatulent, *Passing Wind* and *Breaking Wind*.

For flashy gin palaces owned by wide boys: *Stocks and Blondes*, or *Tax Seavasion*, *Nauti and Nice*, *Nauti Lust*, *A Crewed Interest* or *Miss B'Haven*.

Or *Wannabee Bigger* and *A Loan Again*.

In general: *What's Up Dock?* or *Seas The Day*, *Water Buoy*, *Knot a Care* or, perhaps, *Aquaholic*.

My good friend Lee Wynyard once owned a great fishing boat he named *My Mistress*. We competed in the 2007 NZ Game Fishing Council national championships that year. He wanted all those aboard dressed in team gear and had hats made with the *My Mistress* name and a reclining long–legged and pneumatic blonde beneath it. The same logo appeared on the front of the shirts. On the back, it said 'Mayday, mayday, I'm going down on *My Mistress*.'

THE STORY OF the *Mary Celeste* is the greatest maritime mystery of all time.

The disappearance of the crew remains fascinating and unexplained ever since she was discovered in December 1872 in the Atlantic Ocean, unmanned and apparently abandoned, in perfect weather.

Of one thing there is no doubt — she was cursed with problems from beginning to end.

Three of her captains died, another was sacked after a collision at sea and the last owner/skipper was convicted of insurance fraud after deliberately sinking the ship off Port–au–Prince in Haiti.

The vessel was built in Nova Scotia, Canada, in 1861. She was a 198–tonne brigantine designed for the Atlantic trade and was similar to other merchant sailing ships of the time. She was originally named *Amazon*.

The bad news began just nine days after she was launched, when her first captain Robert McLellan died of pneumonia. He was replaced by John Nutting Parker who struck a fishing boat. While she was in a shipyard in Nova Scotia, a fire broke out mid–ships and Parker was killed. The third skipper was sacked after hitting another vessel in the English Channel.

In 1861, the *Amazon* ran aground at Glace Bay (which gives its name to the Guess Who song *Glace*

Bay Blues) in Nova Scotia, and was substantially damaged. She was salvaged and sold, repaired and refitted and renamed the *Mary Celeste*. The name of the boat is often spelled *Marie Celeste*, but this was a name used by author Sir Arthur Conan Doyle, later of Sherlock Holmes fame, in an early book he wrote based on the ghost ship legend.

On November 5, 1872, *Mary Celeste* left Staten Island, New York, carrying commercial–grade alcohol to Genoa, Italy, where it was to be used to fortify wines. Aboard were seven crew plus the new skipper, Benjamin Spooner Briggs, and his wife, Sarah, and their two–year–old daughter, Sophie.

Curiously, Briggs had gone through maritime school and early seafaring years with the skipper of the boat *Dei Gratia*, which was to find *Mary Celeste* sailing unattended. *Dei Gratia*'s captain, David Reed Morehouse, was a friend of Briggs and the pair had met before leaving New York, no doubt discussing the similar course they were both about to take across the Atlantic Ocean, through the Straits of Gibraltar and into the Mediterranean Sea to Italy.

Dei Gratia left New York on November 15 carrying petroleum. Twenty days later, close to The Azores islands and still 600 miles west of Portugal, crew spotted the *Mary Celeste*, which appeared to be yawing and rolling as if unattended, at about 1pm. They stood off her for two hours, watching with spyglasses, but witnessed no activity at all and so a boarding party was sent.

They found the vessel was devoid of all life. She was not holed or otherwise damaged, though the hold was waist–deep in water.

She had been at sea for a month and had more than six months' food and water on board. Her cargo was virtually untouched as were the personal belongings and valuables of the crew.

Almost all the cargo of 1,701 barrels of alcohol was in good condition, though nine barrels were found to be empty.

Theories abound regarding the fate of the crew — alcohol poisoning, piracy, mutiny, underwater earthquakes, tsunamis, waterspouts and even sea monsters and aliens on UFOs. None has been proved or disproved, despite nearly 140 years of continuing interest and research.

She is often linked to the unusual disappearances of vessels in the Bermuda Triangle, though *Mary Celeste* is not known to have sailed through the area.

Other myths include stories of untouched meals sitting ready to eat on the cabin table and even of hot tea on the stove, though this has been debunked.

Superstitions

It appeared the vessel had been abandoned in a hurry. There was no sign of a struggle, or of any sort of violence. Perhaps the single most powerful clue to what went on was a sturdy rope found tied to the stern, the other end frayed and dragging in the water.

Gone was the ships' lifeboat, the marine chronometer and the sextant, plus all the ship's papers.

Some suggest that the crew of the *Dei Gratia* murdered those on board and told the story of the ghost ship to secure salvage rights. Some say Briggs and Morehouse were in cahoots to defraud the insurers and that Captain Briggs was dropped ashore somewhere and assumed a new identity. But neither Briggs and his family nor the crew of two Americans, four Germans and one Dane, who were all experienced seafarers, were ever seen or heard of again.

Some came up with theories from giant waves to waterspouts which filled the hold with water — she was in no danger of sinking but it was argued that the presence of his wife and daughter made Briggs unusually cautious and all aboard took to a lifeboat.

There was little storm activity in the Atlantic that year. Another master of later times, Captain David Williams, had experienced earthquakes at sea, and suggested that a seaquake erupted below the ship and jarred open nine barrels of alcohol, resulting in the crew abandoning ship for fear of an explosion. Others speculate that Briggs was scared of the effects of fumes from the hold and ordered abandonment. Pirates were suggested, though none had been operating in that area for decades.

An inquiry was held in Gibraltar but reached no conclusion bar the fact the ship was sound. She continued trading but in 1877 her ill–fated saga continued when Henry Winchester–Vinters, father of the then–owner, was drowned when he fell overboard in an accident in Boston Harbour. His son sold the ship.

After eight years of hard times that resulted in little maintenance being done, she was in poor condition when her last master, Captain G.C. Parker, attempted to sink her after over–insuring her cargo of scrap metal and boots. She was scuttled but instead of going down, drifted onto Rochelais Reef, off Tahiti, and stuck fast, allowing investigators to gather evidence to prosecute Parker. No insurance was paid and the boat was sold by the insurers as a shipwreck.

The words 'Mary Celeste' are universally used to this day to describe an unsolvable mystery. The only physical memorial to her is at Spencer's Island, Nova Scotia, where a monument built in the shape of the hull reminds us of the ship and her missing crew.

Superstitions

ANOTHER GREAT seafaring legend is that of the Flying Dutchman, often mistakenly believed to be the name of a boat but in fact the nickname of her captain.

Sailors believe the Dutchman commands an unnamed ghost ship that can never make port and is doomed to roam the oceans forever.

The story originated in 17th century nautical folklore and supposed sightings of the ship are reported vigorously through the 17th and 18th centuries and even into the 20th. The ship is always said to be emitting a ghostly, flickering pale green light. The crew are supposedly dead, walking skeletons.

History records that the master is said by the Dutch to be Captain Van Straaten and that during a violent storm while rounding the Cape of Good Hope, he challenged God Almighty.

God responded to this blasphemy by sentencing Van Straaten to an eternity of meaningless wandering.

The Germans believe the skipper to be a Captain Falkenburg who, according to legend, was said to be cursed to ply the North Sea until Judgement Day after playing dice with the Devil for his own soul.

The boat is always said to be in the distance and moving very quickly. The legend has it that those seeing the boat could contact deceased relatives by shouting messages to her crew, which would then be passed on to souls of the dead. Sightings of the Flying Dutchman are believed to be a portent of death and destruction.

Among those who have claimed to have seen the ship was the young English King George V, while on board the navy gunboat *HMS Bacchante* in 1881. The last officially recorded sighting was reported by the crew of a German U–boat in mid–Atlantic in 1942.

≈ ≈ ≈

THE TRUE 'GHOST SHIPS' of the ocean are those involved in criminal activity ranging from fish poaching to arms, drugs and people smuggling.

Of all these, the case of the *Arctic Star* was perhaps the strangest and it remains unexplained.

The 7000–tonne Russian–manned freighter was en route from Finland to Algeria in northern Africa, supposedly carrying US$1.3 million worth of timber, when it simply vanished for a few weeks in July and early August 2010. It suddenly reappeared on August 17 at Cape Verde, off west Africa, after being tailed by a Russian anti–submarine ship, the *Ladny*.

The Russians claimed the *Arctic Sea* had been raided by pirates and the crew overthrown on July 24 while it was sailing off Scandinavia, the attackers gaining easy access to the boat because they were dressed as police. After recovering the ship, the Russians said they had arrested eight men and charged them with piracy and kidnapping, describing the detainees as two Russians, one Estonian, one Latvian and four 'stateless persons'.

Prior to leaving Russian waters, the *Arctic Sea* had undergone repairs at Kaliningrad, well–known for organised crime gangs that run smuggling rackets.

And after she was found, the head of Russia's Investigative Committee, Alexander Bastrykin, said the *Arctic Sea* may have been carrying a 'secret cargo'. She was sailed back to Russia by crew from the *Ladny* and neither the *Arctic Star* nor the eight detainees have been heard of again.

≈ ≈ ≈

JONAH, THE 'EVIL ANGEL' of all sailors, features in the seafaring legends of the Middle East and is mentioned in both the Hebrew and Christian bibles as well as the Koran.

The stories in each run parallel and change little; Jonah is said to be a prophet for God and distributor of His word but when commanded to go to the city of Ninevah and convince its citizens to change their evil ways, he baulks at the task and instead heads in the opposite direction, taking a sailing ship to the city of Jaffa. He is mid–passage when a fearsome storm descends on the ship. The sailors believe they are cursed and so draw lots to uncover the man carrying the bad luck and Jonah draws the short straw.

After confirming he is the cause of God's wrath in churning the seas, he is thrown overboard, and the waters immediately calm.

Jonah is swallowed by a great fish or a whale. He spends three days and three nights in the fish's stomach and during this time, repents and promises God he will carry out his allotted task.

And so the fish vomits him out onto a beach. God grows a gourd tree over him to protect him from the burning sun while he recovers, and then Jonah redeems himself by completing his mission and so becomes a prophet.

But to this day, to seafarers, 'the luck of Jonah' means bad luck.

≈　　≈　　≈

DEAD SAILORS apparently end up in 'Davy Jones' Locker'. This idiom for 'the bottom of the sea' has been in nautical folklore for at least as long as that of the 'Flying Dutchman', and the two legends were linked for the first time in the *Pirates of the Caribbean* book series which was turned into a series of four movies. The first movie, in 2003, was subtitled *The Curse of the Black Pearl*, the second in 2006 was *Dead Man's Chest*, the third in 2007 was *At World's End* and then *On Stranger Tides* was released in 2011.

The original source of the legend is unknown but in various versions, Davy Jones is either a synonym for the devil, an incompetent sea captain or a pub owner whose hotel was frequented by sailors. In the latter version, Davy Jones throws unconscious drunks into his cellar, from where they are collected by cohorts who sell them to unscrupulous ships masters as crew — the drunks wake up at sea and can do nothing about it.

The earliest known reference of Davy Jones occurs in Scottish author Tobias Smollett's *The Adventures of Peregrine Pickle*, published in 1751. In the story, Jones is described as having saucer eyes, three rows of teeth, horns, a tail, and blue smoke coming from his nostrils.

This same Davy Jones, according to sailors, is the fiend that presides over all the evil spirits of the deep, and is often seen in various shapes, perching among the rigging on the eve of hurricanes, shipwrecks and other disasters to which sea–faring life is exposed. The fiend is a warning of the devoted wretch of death and woe, Smollett wrote.

Other great authors to use references to the legend are Edgar Allan Poe in *King's Pest* in 1835, Herman Melville in the epic *Moby Dick* in 1851, Charles Dickens in *Bleak House* in 1852, Robert Louis Stevenson in *Treasure Island* in 1883 and J.M.Barrie in *Peter Pan and Wendy* in 1904.

In the films, in which Bill Nighy plays Davy Jones, he has a crab claw for his left arm and octopus tentacles for a beard and breathes through a hole in his face. Only the eyes are actually Nighy's, the rest is a 3D computer generation. Davy Jones falls in love with the heathen goddess, Calypso, who gives him the ship *Flying Dutchman* to transport the souls of those lost at sea to 'World's End.' He mutinies, and so is cursed to sail the seven seas forever.

The US Navy song *Anchors Aweigh,* which sailors have sung since the 1920s, refers to Davy Jones in its lyrics.

'Stand, Navy, out to sea, Fight our battle cry;
We'll never change our course,
So vicious foe steer shy–y–y–y.
Roll out the TNT, Anchors Aweigh.
Sail on to victory
And sink their bones to Davy Jones, hooray!'

Superstitions

SOME BOATS CARRY bad luck. Who knows why, but they do.

In mid–2010, the Internet featured pictures of a 37–foot Contender–brand walk–around gamefish boat that had been driven for around 100 metres across what looked like a green field.

The owner had paid US$350,000 for the boat just six hours prior to the grounding. The grass was covered with water at high tide when he decided to take a short cut from one channel on the Florida Everglades flood plain to the next.

But it was just centimetres deep. He was travelling at 28 knots when the props hit dirt. The three 350 horsepower outboards drove her almost to the next deep water, but not quite.

Tugs were called. Four tow ropes snapped before the vessel could be re–floated.

The photographs posted on the Internet by witnesses resulted in disclosure of two further stories regarding the same boat. She had been in and out of the repair shop since launch and her first owner had on–sold her, sick of the continuing mechanical and hull problems.

The second owner took five mates to The Bahamas to contest a fishing tournament but at 1.45am on the morning after they arrived, the boat was stolen from the marina. A GPS tracing device installed on the boat allowed insurance investigators to trace her to Andros Island, 160kms away. And so she was sold to owner number three, who ran her aground.

≈   ≈   ≈

AMONGST THE most well–known no–no's at sea are shooting albatross and taking bananas on board, especially when fishing.

The first of these superstitions comes from the poem *The Rime of the Ancyent Marinere* by Samuel Taylor Coleridge, written in 1797. The second is a practicality concerning food storage during long voyages in olden times, but modified by Hawaiian gamefishermen.

The poem may have been inspired by Captain James Cook's second voyage to the South Seas, during which he twice ventured into Antarctic waters and it mirrors a scene in a book from Coleridge's time in which a sea captain shoots a black albatross that has been following his ship.

In Coleridge's poem, the albatross is believed by the mariner to be to blame for the foul winds that push them towards Antarctica. When he shoots it, the boat gets favourable winds and moves north to the equator. And here, the boat stops dead on 'a painted ocean' without a breath of wind, and so the crew run out of food and drink. The long poem includes the widely-known stanza: 'Water, water, everywhere, And all the boards did shrink; Water, water, everywhere, Nor any drop to drink.'

The crew blame the shooting of the albatross for their plight and hang the dead bird around the neck of the mariner — hence the seafarers' saying about a bad boat.

The ship encounters a ghostly vessel and the mariner meets Death and Night–mare Life–in–Death, who are rolling dice to gamble for the souls of the crew. Life–in–Death wins the mariner's soul and so in penance for his crime of shooting the albatross, he must endure a fate worse than death, and is forced to wander the earth and tell his story to teach a lesson to those he meets.

Early Polynesian ocean voyagers soon worked out that bananas, although a great source of protein and energy, ripen very quickly and then give off a chemical agent that encourages other stored foods to ripen. As a result, the entire supply of food for a long trip might quickly go rotten, and so bananas were not taken on voyages of more than a day. This practice spread to the European explorers.

Then in the 1960s, Hawaiian skippers of game boats started the practice of banning bananas as they were bad luck for fishing. It may have been a gimmick or the result of a coincidental run of bad days for one particular boat on which a deckhand regularly ate bananas — choose your version of the story as the origin is not precise.

Anyway, it was not long before Hawaiian game boats featured stickers with the symbol from the movie *Ghostbusters*, a red circle with a slash across it, but with the ghost inside the circle replaced by a banana. The charter skippers wore T-shirts with the same emblem. And because Hawaii at that time was the Mecca for gamefishermen, the practice quickly spread to the mainland United States and then around the world. To this day, there are skippers, recreational and professional, who swear you will not catch fish if there are bananas on board.

One wag suggested rolling two superstitions into one. His explanation of the theory that the renaming of a boat and bringing bananas on board a ship are both bad luck: 'Try calling your wife by a different name and eating bananas while getting intimate.'

'God save thee, ancient mariner, from the fiends that plague thee thus. Why look'st thou so?
With my crossbow, I shot the albatross.'
– Samuel Taylor Coleridge, poet (1772–1834).

Stuff–ups

'There is no dilemma compared with that of the deep–sea diver who hears the message from the ship above, "Come up at once. We are sinking."'
– Robert Cooper, American self–help author.

Most small boaties have at some stage been left land–locked by their own mistakes. I wish I had a dollar for every time I've left something behind and didn't realise that until I got on board.

You know the stuff — bait, hats, rain jackets, favourite rods, the new lure, the sunglasses, the tasty lunch made the night before that you know is still sitting in the fridge and won't be there when you get home. And the keys.

Early one morning, I was going fishing in Auckland with television fishing show host Geoff Thomas and the All Black Ali Williams. When we got to the boat ramp, Geoff realised he had left the boat keys on his kitchen table in Mt Eden and so we waited at Okahu Bay while they were fetched.

Then there are the unwanted things that are aboard. Glen Eden mate Alan Jessop got to the ramp one day to find the family cat distressed after its sleep in the carport had been disrupted by a bumpy trip in the boat behind the car. He had to take pussy home before getting on the water.

≈　　　≈　　　≈

MISTAKING WATER and fuel filling points, and putting diesel into petrol tanks and vice–versa, are relatively common occurrences.

It's an expensive business no matter which you do. The tanks have to be pumped and the contaminated fluid disposed of at great expense. And no amount of flushing will ever completely rid a water storage tank of the taste of diesel.

I've got a mate–of–a–mate who was filling his brand–spanking new boat for the first time. He pulled into the gas station, stuck the pump into the filler hole and set the trigger on.

After a few minutes wait, he noticed the fuel guage had spun up to $150 and there was a strong smell of gasoline in the air. That was when he realised he had put the fuel hose into a rod holder and all the petrol had been splashing into the bottom of the boat — about 80–odd litres of it, emitting explosive fumes around a petrol station.

That required a major salvage operation. He was not popular.

≈   ≈   ≈

THE GREATEST SIN for a naval commander is to lose his ship, and the greatest embarrassment is to put his vessel in danger of loss.

Yet this happens reasonably regularly and despite all the fancy technology these vessels boast.

It is uncanny how many of these accidents occur after the ship has been serviced.

On October 22, 2010, Britain's new nuclear attack submarine with the somewhat ironic name of *HMS Astute*, as it turned out, ran aground on a sand and silt bar off the Isle of Skye, Scotland.

The submarine cost about £1 billion and had sonar equipment with a theoretical range of 3,000 nautical miles. But after having maintenance and leaving her base in Faslane at Clyde, she ran into a sucking sludge off the Isle of Skye and was stuck fast for six hours while waiting for a high tide to provide some lift. Ballast was ejected to lower her weight and she re–floated.

The navy insisted no nuclear–armed Tomahawk cruise missiles were on board at the time.

The same assurance was given when the frigate *HMS Trafalgar* went aground in the same area in 2002. *Trafalgar*'s first and second–in–command later admitted charges of carelessness.

The United States Navy was deeply disturbed when the destroyer *USS Barry* was towed onto a sandbank in Samsun Harbour, Turkey, while manoeuvring prior to departure to support troops in the Iraq war in October 2008.

But at least that was the Turkish tow boat's fault and no damage was caused.

The Americans were far more distressed when the US$1 billion guided missile cruiser *Port Royal* ran aground on a reef off the main Hawaiian island of Oahu in February 2009. The boat was stuck for three days, defying attempts to tow her free, until the navy finally pumped out fuel and water and took half her complement of 360 to shore to lighten her payload by 150 tonnes. Like *Astute*, she had just been serviced, spending four months in the docks at Pearl Harbour before the accident.

Rear Admiral Joe Walsh, the deputy commander of

the US Pacific Fleet, was bristling when he said the shoal hit by the *Port Royal* was known to the navy and she had grounded in only seven metres of water.

'Clearly, the ship is not where the ship should have been. The investigation will determine exactly why the ship got to the point where she was in shoal water,' Walsh said as repeated tow attempts failed in the first two days.

≈   ≈   ≈

THE AVAILABILITY of all types of information — including military secrets — on the Internet means no one was surprised when various 'news' sites began reporting that a US naval vessel had narrowly avoided running aground on rocks. The stories blamed the near-miss on the arrogance and stupidity of its commanding officer.

One site told the yarn as follows:

'This is the transcript of an actual radio conversation between a US naval ship and Canadian authorities off the coast of Newfoundland in October 1995.

'The radio conversation was released by the Chief of Naval Operations on October 10, 1995.'

US Ship: Please divert your course 0.5 degrees to the south to avoid a collision.

Canadian reply: Recommend you divert your course 15 degrees to the south to avoid a collision.

US Ship: This is the captain of a US Navy ship. I say again, divert your course.

Canadian reply: No. I say again, you divert YOUR course!

US Ship: THIS IS THE AIRCRAFT CARRIER *USS CORAL SEA*, WE ARE A LARGE WARSHIP OF THE US NAVY. DIVERT YOUR COURSE NOW!

Canadian reply: This is a lighthouse. Your call.

When the story began to circulate worldwide, the details changed, with some versions having the lighthouse in Ireland or Scotland, and some versions naming the ship as the *USS Missouri* or *USS Nimitz*.

By 2004, an elaborate video had been made by persons unknown, featuring the same ship–to–shore dialogue, but in this version, the warship was a destroyer.

Officially, no such incident ever occurred and the story is now considered to be an urban myth.

≈ ≈ ≈

THE DOLDRUMS is the name given to the 'intertropical convergence zone' where the winds of the northern and southern hemispheres meet and effectively cancel each other out, just north of the equator in the Indian, Pacific and Atlantic Oceans.

It's also the scene of a major environmental stuff up — the 'Great Garbage Swirl'.

High temperature in The Doldrums means the only air movement goes straight to the upper atmosphere from where it then disperses north and south. This creates flat–calm conditions and a total lack of wind, conditions which sometimes becalmed sailing ships for weeks at a time.

The unusual conditions also created the 'Great Garbage Swirl' that exists mid–Pacific between the United States and Japan, where tens of thousands of tonnes of plastic and other rubbish washed or thrown into the sea has conglomerated into a maritime rubbish dump that circles continuously on currents but does not disperse.

Today, the term doldrums is more frequently used to describe the demeanour of someone who is tired, listless, or inactive.

≈   ≈   ≈

LANCE PANIORA is an accomplished fisherman having been taught by his dad while growing up on the Hokianga Harbour and then joining his father as a commercial fisherman.

But the pair didn't get on, as is often the case with dads and their lads, so Lance went south to Auckland to make a living as a charter operator on the Hauraki Gulf. He was a good one. And so we booked him repeatedly and always came home with a feed of fish.

Lance's routine was to launch his six–man trailer boat at the Westhaven ramp and then pick the clients up from the wharf at the nearby petrol station, where they could make any last–minute purchases of drinks and a pie, bait or hooks.

After we loaded, I said to him, 'So you don't need petrol?' No, he replied, he'd filled up after the last trip, and so off we went.

Heading back, his boat *Reel Passion* ran out of fuel and sputtered to a stop just a few minutes from the Harbour Bridge. He had to call out the coastguard who were only a short trip away in Mechanics Bay.

They all knew Lance and of course couldn't help but take the Mickey. 'That's your one free call–out this year,' one said, 'and don't worry, we won't call the media.'

'I will,' I replied, 'I work for the *Herald*.' I haven't told that story until now — and only because Lance is no longer in the business.

Disasters

'*The sea finds out everything you did wrong.*'
— *Francis Stokes, trans–oceanic solo sailor (1926–2008).*

Rarely does a boat sink due to one, solitary reason such as an equipment failure or one poor decision by the skipper.

Usually a combination of factors leads to disaster — poor boat design, mistakes in preparation, failure of old or untested gear, the use of outdated charts — and these are compounded by bad decisions by skippers and bad weather.

The recipe for disaster is completed with simple oversights — such as failure of communications gear due to low batteries, failure to file trip reports, carrying no emergency locator beacon (EPIRB) and too few lifejackets.

Weather shows no favours to vessels, big or small.

≈   ≈   ≈

THE INTERISLAND car, train and passenger ferry *Wahine* went down in atrocious weather when it hit Barrett Reef while attempting to enter Wellington Harbour on the morning of April 10, 1968.

For those who belive in superstition, there were early warnings of what would happen to her. Her fate was also a classic illustration of how it is usually not one, but rather a string of issues that precede disaster.

The first ship named *Wahine* sank after hitting a reef. Built for the interisland service prior to World War One, it was carrying troops to the Korean War in 1951 when it grounded on a reef in the Arafura Sea, north of Darwin.

The captain of the ill–fated second *Wahine*, Hector Robertson, had served on the first *Wahine* as a deck officer.

Departure from Lyttleton on the night of April 6 was delayed by a string of problems including the late arrival of a train from Invercargill, a power failure on the wharf and difficulty removing the span via which passengers went on board.

Wahine eventually set off into a 15 knot westerly

wind with 610 passengers, including 41 children, and 125 crew. Less than 12 hours later, the seas were being driven by a 50 knot southerly that was pushing a rising swell. The reason was the formation and quick change of direction of a 'rogue' cyclone to the north of New Zealand, a 970 millibar depression that was sucking wind into its centre.

By the time *Wahine* approached Pencarrow Head at the entrance to Wellington Harbour at dawn, the winds and seas were still rising. It was worst in the narrow harbour mouth.

Driving rain lashed the ship, reducing visibility almost to nil as she came into Chaffers Passage, the harbour entrance channel. Then the ship's radar failed. The captain ordered lookouts fore and aft.

Suddenly, and without warning, the ship lurched violently to port. She would not respond to the helm or to full astern drive — the swells were so large and so close together they were constantly lifting the middle of the ship up with both ends poking free of the water and the screws turning uselessly.

Robertson decided to go full ahead and try to turn back out to sea. At that instant, a 'rogue wave' estimated at 13 metres rolled over *Wahine*, smashing glass on the bridge and swamping the bridge cabin with water. Robertson was thrown 20 metres across the width of the cockpit and smashed his head. He told the subsequent inquest: 'I picked myself up, bruised from one end to the other. Then I heard the awful shrieking of the wind and I thought, "We're rushing straight for Barrett Reef at 16 knots." I knew we had about one and a half minutes before we would go ashore. The noise of the wind was so bad we had to shout to make ourselves heard. We could feel nothing, see nothing and hear only the scream of the wind.'

Next came the call of 'rocks ahead', followed almost immediately by 'rocks astern.'

'There was no way of getting out of it,' Robertson said later. 'She was picked up bodily and thrown onto the reef.'

An SOS call was sent at 7.02am but weather conditions were so bad, the ship's distress was not understood. Serious weather–related incidents on shore were keeping emergency services busy.

Anchors were deployed to hold *Wahine* upright in place and they did so successfully for several hours.

The tug *Tapuhi* arrived and attached a cable to *Wahine* and tried to tow her off, but the line snapped. Then the windlass on *Tapuhi* broke.

By this time, at about noon, the storm was abating rapidly and the wind had dropped to 40 knots as high tide approached. The harbour, though, contained too much wind–driven water and as conditions levelled in Cook Strait, it drained out in a rush.

At 12.56pm, *Wahine* lurched violently to starboard and the order was given to prepare to abandon ship.

This news shocked those ashore, who until then had believed the *Wahine* and those aboard were grounded but in no peril.

Suddenly, they had to organise a major sea rescue from scratch. They were fortunate that by this time the local radio station 2ZB had broadcast callers' reports of passengers being seen going over the side into liferafts. Local boating and surf club members turned out in force, as did shoreline residents.

Rescue boats ranged from rubber inflatables to jet–boats, surf boats and yachts, as well as the Harbour Board tugs and official emergency services including police and coastguard.

This rescue effort helped restrict the death toll to 51 when it could have been far worse. Survivors were picked up off Pencarrow Coast at Camp Bay and Hinds Point by local residents and taken to their homes, the Hutt Hospital or the local RSA clubrooms and primary school.

In the aftermath, Captain Robertson, his Chief Officer and the Chief Engineer were charged with offences alleging they caused the loss of the ship and subsequent loss of life due to 'wrongful acts or defaults'. After a 26–day hearing in the Wellington District Court at which 81 witnesses gave evidence, all charges were dismissed.

≈   ≈   ≈

ROLL–ON, ROLL–OFF car ferries are by far the ships most prone to sinking.

They have been involved in some of the worst maritime disasters in countries including Great Britain, Belgium, Scandinavia, Egypt, China and other Asian nations and the Pacific Islands. Dubbed Ro–Ro ferries, they can roll right over in less than a minute if water floods the vehicle decks.

The various reasons for these tragedies are epic tales of bad seamanship and bad company management. The rescue operations produced both heroic and pitiful tales. Conspiracy theories abound regarding some of the sinkings, especially the worst of all time, that of the *Estonia*. She sank off Finland on September 28, 1994, with the loss of 852 lives, the worst maritime disaster of the 20th century.

The ferry was built in Sweden in 1980 and named the *Viking Sally*. The name changed after she was sold to the newly–established Estonian Government which formed after the break–up of the Soviet Union. She was en route from Tallin, Estonia, to Stockholm during what was later described as an 'average autumn Baltic Sea storm', with winds of 40 knots and four–metre waves.

At 1am, passengers and crew heard a loud bang from the bow. An interior inspection was made but nothing was found to be wrong. But more banging continued. At 1.15am, the banging became consistent, and then it stopped. Immediately, the vessel took on a 30 degree list to starboard. By 1.30am, she had rolled over.

A mayday was transmitted in Estonian. The Finnish radio operator who received it did not understand the seriousness of the situation and diverted another ship to check on *Estonia*. And so it was 2.30am before emergency rescue helicopters were scrambled and they did not arrive at the scene until 3.05am.

The Baltic is the world's busiest shipping lane, with more than 2,000 vessels at sea at any one time. More lives might have been saved had the rescue call been relayed immediately. The water temperature was 10 degrees and many died of hypothermia.

Ships picked up 34 survivors and helicopters saved 104 more. The survivors of the sinking were all from the upper decks, mostly young, physically strong, and male. Seven people over 55 years of age survived.

No survivors were younger than 12. The dead included 501 Swedes, 285 Latvians and a wide variety of other nationalities. No attempt was ever made to recover their bodies from inside the wreck.

An investigation found that the ship was built for coastal travel, not open ocean work. She had left port listing slightly because of poor cargo distribution. The bang heard at 1am was one of the locks on the bow visor giving way under the force of the storm–driven sea. The next bangs were the remaining locks successively severing and when the noise stopped, it was because the visor and bow ramp had been ripped free, allowing water to rush in. The captain and crew did not slow the boat from her usual speed of 15 knots after the first bang, nor did they investigate the subsequent banging.

She went down in 85 metres off Finland's Uno Island. No salvage was ever attempted and several countries including Estonia, Sweden, Finland and Great Britain signed an agreement that no divers would be allowed to go to the wreck. It was covered in a layer of pebbles.

This led to speculation, media coverage, a book and a movie that featured claims of espionage. Britain's MI6 had supposedly purchased Russian–made weapons to keep abreast of that country's military capabilities, or so the story went. The weapons were being shipped to the American CIA, so the Russian Secret Service sank the vessel.

≈   ≈   ≈

THE INVESTIGATION into the sinking of the *Herald of Free Enterprise* just after she left port in Belgium revealed a string of disastrous errors. The ship was built for England–based Townsend Thorensen, a subsidiary of the P&O company, specifically designed for the Dover–to–Calais run.

On March 6, 1987, she loaded at the Belgian port of Zeebrugge. At Dover and Calais, two levels of vehicle access allowed all car decks to be loaded. But at Zeebrugge, there was just one and the lower car deck was empty.

To compensate and distribute weight, the bow ballast tanks were filled with water. She sailed at 9pm, with 459 passengers, most of whom were English and readers of *The Sun* newspaper which had organised the trip for them. They were accompanied by 80 crew, three buses, 47 trucks and 81 cars.

One kilometre from shore, and seconds after the throttles were opened to take her to her cruising speed of 18 knots, water flooded into the lower vehicle deck, and within 45 seconds she had rolled 90 degrees. Luckily, she grounded on a sandbar.

In the panic that followed, 193 people died, mostly of hypothermia in the 3 degrees water. Fortunately, the Belgian Navy was conducting an exercise in the area and was quickly on the scene to save hundreds of lives.

A British army corporal gave a harrowing account later to an inquest, describing how he was one of many trying to climb a rope ladder out of the sea and onto the side of the ship. A young man pulled himself halfway up to safety but then froze in panic, unable to move up or down. After several minutes, and with people swimming in the freezing water, the corporal climbed the ladder and pushed the man off so others could be saved. He was never seen again. The corporal was not admonished.

The subsequent inquiry in London found that the vessel's loading doors had been left open. The boatswain who was supposed to close them was asleep in his cabin. The first officer who was supposed to check the boatswain's work didn't because loading had run late and he was anxious to depart. The captain did not check, as was required, that the first officer had ensured the doors were shut and locked. There was no warning light or signal to the wheelhouse to show the doors were open. The investigating judge found a 'disease of sloppiness and negligence' throughout the company. P&O changed the name of the company and painted over the 'TT' logo on the *Herald*'s sister ships, the *Spirit of Free Enterprise* and the *Pride of Free Enterprise*. In April 1987, the *Herald* was re–floated, towed to shipyards and refitted ready for sale. But after a long tender process there were no buyers and she was sailed to Taiwan and cut up for scrap.

The death toll was the worst for an English–operated ship in peacetime.

≈   ≈   ≈

IN 1953, 130 people drowned when the car ferry *Princess Victoria* rolled and sank during a storm in the Irish Sea while en route from Stranraer, Scotland, to Larne in Northern Ireland.

Nearly 1,000 lives were lost when the Egyptian car ferry *Salam Boccacio* sank 60 kilometres off the Red Sea port of Hurghada while on the 200km trip from Dubah to Safarga.

On board were 1,498, many returning from the annual pilgrimage to the Hajj festival at Mecca in Saudi Arabia.

In November 2009, most of the 300 passengers and

40 crew aboard the car ferry *Dashun* were killed when fire broke out during a storm off the coast of China. It is believed an LPG gas tank on a vehicle exploded, igniting a fire which quickly spread through the ship, forcing people to jump overboard.

Only 36 survivors found lifeboats. One man, Ma Shuchi, swam the 9kms to shore.

≈   ≈   ≈

THE PACIFIC ISLANDS have long been the final workplace for many ships sold cheaply after a long time at sea. The *Princess Ashika* was one such vessel.

On August 5, 2009, she went down in the Ha'apai Islands group off Tonga. Late that night, she quickly listed badly and then rolled and sank within minutes after cargo shifted in heavy weather.

More than 100 drowned. The 54 survivors were all on the open deck.

An inquiry was told the ship was unfit for its role, was rusty and poorly maintained, and that advice on these issues had been ignored. The owner, the company and three employees were charged with and convicted of manslaughter.

In 2003, the *Princess Ashika*'s sister ship *Ovalau* sank off Fiji after she sprang a leak and her pumps could not cope. She took several hours to go down and the *Ashika* was sent to off–load passengers.

Off Thailand, a car ferry with 561 people on board went down in flat–calm seas in the middle of the day. The *King Cruiser,* which made regular trips between Phuket and Ko Phi Phi Island, steamed straight onto the well–known Anemone Reef and her bottom was ripped out.

Rumours abounded regarding the reason. Some said the skipper was drunk, others suggested his daughter was steering at the time. Nothing was proved and as no one was killed, the inquiry into the sinking was closed.

≈   ≈   ≈

THE LOSS OF THE passenger liner *Titanic* holds as much fascination today as it did when it went down in April 1912. It is a magnet for historians and speculators, conspiracy theorists and would–be salvagers alike.

There are several reasons. Firstly, the ship was the largest afloat at that time, being 269 metres long and 28 metres wide. It was the most opulently appointed liner in the world. It featured all the latest technology, including water–tight bulkheads that led to her being described as 'unsinkable'.

Secondly, stories circulated of sailors and passengers who boarded in Southampton but after foreseeing their deaths, they jumped ship when she stopped in Ireland before departing for New York.

Thirdly, a pulp magazine on sale prior to the *Titanic*'s departure featured a fictional story about a huge liner hitting an iceberg.

And there was talk the ship was cursed. Some blamed the curse on the ship's Protestant owners and workforce at the Belfast shipyard that built her, saying their prejudice against Catholics would be punished. One shipyard worker was said to have painted 'even God can't sink this ship' on the bottom of her hull.

Titanic was on the fourth day of her trip to America on a moonless night when she hit an iceberg while steaming at 21 knots in perfectly calm, flat conditions. The 11.40pm collision ripped a 90–metre gash down her side, effectively making the water–tight compartment system useless.

When the order was given to abandon ship, no one acted with a sense of urgency because nothing appeared to be wrong. But as a list developed, passengers rushed for the lifeboats only to discover the ship had too few.

The lifeboats could carry only 1,178 people when the ship had 2,227 on board.

As passengers and crew went into the freezing sea,

or were trapped inside the stricken ship, the death toll rose to 1,517. The toll was highest among those in third class cabins in the ship's bowels, and amongst the crew, of whom 24% survived.

Of those travelling second class, the survival rate was 40% and of first class passengers, travelling on the upper decks, it was 60%.

After 2am, the bow went underwater, the stern raised in the air and then the ship broke in two and both halves sank.

Captain Edward John Smith, who had been in the radio room calling for assistance, walked to the bridge and went down with his ship.

The liner *Californian* was nearby but did not respond to calls for help. *Carpathia* came from 89kms away, arriving at 4am, and collected the survivors in lifeboats, but those in the −2 degrees water had died of hypothermia.

A stewardess, Violet Jessop, would survive a second shipwreck on *Titanic's* sister ship *Britannic*. It was converted for use as a hospital ship during World War One, hit a mine and sank off Greece in 1916.

The last *Titanic* survivor was Millivia Dean who was nine years old at the time and passed away in 2009, on the 98th anniversary of the launch of *Titanic's* hull.

The ship wreckage was not found until September

1985, in water 4kms deep and 600kms south–east of Newfoundland. Since then, ownership of the wreck has been contested in court, with an exhibitions company awarded ownership and salvage rights in 1994 by a Virginian court. Fifteen years later, the courts were still dealing with claims and counter–claims.

More than 6,000 artefacts have been recovered and these are held at the National Maritime Museum in Greenwich, England.

≈   ≈   ≈

MANY BELIEVE THAT the early history of a boat can show portents of its future and precursors of disaster. The story of the steamship carrier *Edmund Fitzgerald* gives life to such theories.

The *Edmund Fitzgerald* was carrying iron ore from Superior, Wisconsin, across Lake Superior to the steel mills of Detroit, Michigan, when 'the gales of November came early', as the singer Gordon Lightfoot puts it in his song that carries the ship's name.

To this day, the exact fate of the ship remains a mystery but she went down in a storm with the loss of 29 lives, still the worst maritime disaster in the history of shipping on America's Great Lakes.

She was built in 1958 for the Northwestern Life

Assurance Company of Wisconsin and named for the company's chairman. Northwestern had ordered 'the biggest ship on the lakes'. The St Lawrence Seaway, which controls the locks between the Great Lakes, limits ship size to 223 metres long and 23 metres wide — and those were her measurements.

The launch ceremony had some anxious moments, as Fitzgerald's wife failed in her first two attempts to break the traditional bottle of Champagne on her bow. When she smashed it on the third shot, and workers tried to let the ship slide backwards into the water, some of the blocks holding her jammed around the keel. It took 36 minutes to free her and when released, she shot back unevenly, listed badly as she hit the water and smashed violently against a pier before righting.

She had run aground on Lake Superior in 1969, collided with the freighter *SS Hakelaga* in 1970, and hit lock walls in both 1973 and 1974.

At 8,713 tonnes empty, and capable of carrying 26,000 tonnes of ore, she quickly earned the nicknames 'The Big Fitz' and 'Mighty Fitz.'

A commonly accepted theory is that the boat sprang plates in her hull, allowing water to enter the front compartments. She went down like a stone.

≈   ≈   ≈

MECHANICAL FAILURE caused the world's two worst submarine disasters — one from the United States and one from Russia — when the 129 men aboard the *USS Thresher* and 118 on the Russian vessel *Kursk* were all killed.

Each was a showcase submarine of its time. *Thresher* was pride of the US fleet of nuclear–powered attack subs when it was launched in 1960.

But, as with so many stories in this book, portents of doom were there for those who look for them.

The *Thresher* had continuing problems with her power reactor and the diesel generator that supplied electricity to the boat. In Puerto Rico in 1961, she was evacuated and her reactor shut down because temperatures inside had hit 60 degrees — too hot for crew to operate. Another sub was sent to help power her up again.

When entering port in Florida in 1963, she was struck by a tugboat and her ballast tanks were damaged. That required months to repair and on her return to sea, deep–dive trials were ordered. She was 190 nautical miles north–east of Cape Cod in Massachusetts when a brief radio message reported a minor problem.

She was never heard from again. She sank in 2,400 metres of water and broke into six parts.

The nukes aboard made salvage an imperative for

the United States. Subsequent investigation into the sinking found it was caused by a burst saltwater–carrying ballast pipe. A joint had been brazed rather than welded.

The K–141 *Kursk* was named for the Russian town where the largest tank battle of all time took place between the homeland defenders and the German invaders in 1943. It was launched in 1997, boasting to be the largest nuclear attack submarine ever built, a claim that remains true today. It was 154 metres in length and 15 metres high; about the height of a four–storey building. It had an outer case made from a blend of high–grade chromium and stainless steel that was designed to defeat the usual steel sub–seeking sonar gear. This was 8.5cm thick.

Two metres inside the outer case was the sub's inner core, made of steel 50cm thick.

The *Kursk* tracked the United States' Sixth Fleet as it patrolled the Mediterranean during the war in Kosovo in 1999–2000, working undetected, according to the Russians, and after months at sea was ordered to port at Severmorsk. After service and resupply, she put to sea on August 12, 2000. When 135kms into the Barents Sea, she sank in 108 metres of water, blown apart due to a chemical reaction caused by a rusted torpedo casing.

The concentrated hydrogen peroxide used as propellant in the torpedo escaped and was somehow ignited by a spark, causing an explosion that was measured by seismographs as 2.2 on the Richter scale. Two minutes later, a far bigger blast, measuring 4.2, shook the vessel as five of seven torpedo warheads detonated.

Despite the force of the explosion, it is believed many crew survived it, protected in a separated and sealed bow section. Rescue offers by the British and Norwegians, who had experience of deep−dive operations in the North Sea, were rejected. Eventually the Russians hired a Dutch barge, the *Giant 4,* to retrieve four of the five parts into which *Kursk* was blown. The last, the bow section containing crew, was taken apart by explosives.

The Russian president at the time, Vladimir Putin, was on holiday with his family at a Black Sea dacha (seaside cabin) at Sochi when news of the incident broke. He remained on holiday for five more days before returning to Moscow.

≈   ≈   ≈

THE ANNUAL SYDNEY to Hobart yacht race is nicknamed Hell on High Water because of the southern storms that roll northwards to make life miserable, and progress over the 1,167kms slow.

It ran for 53 years with the loss of just two lives; one sailor swept overboard in gale–force winds in 1984, and another who died of head injuries received when a mast snapped in 1989.

But in 1998, that toll quadrupled.

The race starts at lunchtime on Boxing Day in the sheltered calm of Sydney Harbour and ends with a slow tack up the largely windless Derwent River to the Tasmanian capital.

No one had any reason to expect hurricane–force winds as the last race instructions were given prior to departure, and the fleet of 115 contestants set off into gentle westerlies.

But by the evening of December 27, the sea was building and the wind rising. A depression had formed south of Tasmania and was deepening rapidly and moving northward.

By the time the boats got to Eden, at the lower end of the New South Wales coastline, snow was falling on land and at sea the swell was topping 12 metres and winds were up to 70 knots, or 145kmh.

Many boats withdrew and headed for shelter. Five were sunk, one by a waterspout. Six sailors were drowned. They were Phillip Skeggs and Bruce Guy (on *Business Post Naiad*), John Dean, James Lawler and Michael Bannister (on *Winston Churchill*), and Glyn Charles (on *Sword of Orion*).

Only 44 of the 115 boats finished. Thanks to the Royal Australian Navy, which sent 27 vessels to the rescue, and the Air Force, which picked sailors from their stricken yachts in atrocious conditions, 55 more lives were saved.

It is the largest peacetime marine rescue in Australia's history.

American computer billionaire Larry Ellison's boat *Oracle* won the event.

The coroner's inquest found those at race headquarters were 'observers' rather than 'organisers' and that they failed to relay urgent weather warnings or put the race on hold.

Of race manager Phil Thompson, the coroner said: 'Mr Thompson's inability to appreciate the problems when they arose and his inability to appreciate them at the time of giving his evidence causes me concern that (he) may not appreciate such problems as they arise in the future.'

The day after the inquest findings were released Phil Thompson resigned from the race committee.

≈　　　≈　　　≈

Disasters

THE WORST YACHT racing disaster of all time occurred during the 23rd running of the biennial Fastnet, from Cowes on the Isle of Wight, around the lighthouse that marks the most southern point of Ireland and back, a 608 nautical mile journey.

Again, it was unpredicted hurricane–force winds that caused the trouble. There were 335 yachts competing in what was the fifth and final leg of the Admiral's Cup international series in August 1979.

As in the Sydney–Hobart tragedy, the racers were well at sea when the weather suddenly blew up to produce wind and swell that had not been predicted.

Twenty five yachts sank or were abandoned while 69 other entrants pulled out of the race and headed for shelter. Fifteen sailors drowned. A mass rescue effort saved the lives of 125 others. The search and rescue effort involved harbour tugs, a fishing trawler and an ocean–going tanker as well as six Royal Navy vessels and 12 military helicopters.

The race winner was *Condor of Bermuda* which broke the existing race record by eight hours, finishing in 71hrs 25mins. First on corrected time was *Tenacious*, owned and skippered by the American media magnate Ted Turner.

≈   ≈   ≈

NEW ZEALAND'S worst yacht racing disaster occurred in January 1956 when 22 boats entered a Wellington to Lyttleton race held to commemorate the Canterbury Centennial.

They were hit by bad southerly gales after leaving Cook Strait. Two boats, the *Husky* and *Argo*, were lost and the 10 men aboard were all drowned. All but one of the remaining fleet, the *Tawhiri* from Nelson, turned for shelter and so *Tawhiri* won.

In June 1983, tragedy struck as boats were returning from the racing of the annual Auckland to Suva, Fiji, race that has been held every year since 1956.

Again, an unexpectedly deep depression hit and as two frontal systems squashed into each other, the returning yachts were caught in the squeeze.

Two of those on the boat *Lionheart* were suffering serious sea–sickness and so instead of staying well out to sea and continuing down the coast towards a large safe harbour at the Bay of Islands, the crew opted to go for the narrow entrance at Whangaroa, where barely 200 metres separates steep cliffs that drop to the sea.

As they tried to run the gap they were picked up by a large wave and lost steerage. The yacht was driven onto rocks and smashed to pieces and seven lives were lost.

≈   ≈   ≈

Disasters

NEW ZEALAND'S worst–ever maritime disaster was the grounding of the naval steam–sailship *HMS Orpheus* on the Manukau Harbour bar in 1863, with the loss of 189 lives. The early background of *Orpheus* gives more weight to the theory of premonitions of disaster.

The near–new Royal Navy ship was an early combination of sail and steam–driven engine and was sent to New Zealand at the height of the Maori Land Wars loaded with troops, field supplies and ammunition to reinforce the British positions.

After a string of captaincy errors, which included following an old chart, taking the wrong course through the treacherous bar crossing area and ignoring the frantic semaphore (hoisted flags) signalling from the land, she grounded on a sandbank.

Of 259 on board, 189 died. Three separate inquiries tried to lay blame on the Manukau signalman Thomas Wing and his then 18–year–old son who was assisting him.

But eventually the truth came out — a navy deserter who had been recaptured in Sydney was the only man on board to have crossed the bar before but when he warned the captain they were taking a bad course he was ignored. Wing also saw the ship heading too far south and initially signalled *Orpheus* by flag that she should head north, later changing that to 'Stop, do not take the bar.' His instructions were ignored by the master, Commodore W.F. Burnett.

Queerly, Burnett's remains washed ashore 17 days later not far from the wreck site, fully clothed in dress uniform. He was the third skipper of *Orpheus* to die on board in the six brief years she was afloat.

The first captain, Robert McLellan, contracted pneumonia immediately after she left London on her first voyage and died just nine days after taking charge.

The second, John Parker, was killed in a fire mid–ships while repairs were being made following a collision with a fishing boat. Then there was Burnett.

To this day, timber from *Orpheus* is occasionally exposed by the massive wind and wave–driven sand movement that occurs on the west coast, off Auckland.

A monument to the deceased sits atop the hill at Cornwallis.

≈   ≈   ≈

Sinkings

'*Should you find yourself in a chronically leaking boat, energy devoted to changing vessels is likely to be more productive than energy devoted to patching leaks.*'
— *Warren Buffett, American investor/philanthropist (1930–).*

The majority of recreational boat sinkings occur at dockside. That means it is easy to determine the cause because vessels are raised and can be inspected.

History reveals the most common reasons for boats to sink at dockside, as follows:

☐ A fitting below the waterline failed.

☐ Rain or snow added too much weight.

☐ A failed fitting above the waterline.

☐ Improper docking — a boat being caught under a dock with a rising tide, for instance.

☐ Fires and explosions.

When vessels sink while underway, it is usually far more difficult to determine the cause as the craft are usually lost. Insurance investigations show that the most common cause of sinking while underway is poor vessel design.

Badly designed cockpits are the most common reason powerboats sink.

Outboard–powered vessels are the ones most often swamped, because they have engine cut–outs which are a few centimetres above the water and suffer electrical failure when water comes inboard over the gunwales or transom.

Other problems are:

☐ Hull damage due to collision, or striking objects as diverse as a reef to a channel marker.

☐ Bilge pumps failing. In yachts and powerboats, bad examples of plumbing, such as poor installation of the head, sink and drains, or inadequate bilge pumps and battery systems, can all cause disaster. So can blocked pumping outlets, failed hull fittings and hose failure.

☐ Over weighting. A 450–litre fuel tank holds almost 320 kgs of fuel. The fuel can change the trim of an eight–metre boat by at least five centimetres. When the tank is toward the stern, the change may be even greater.

☐ Improper loading with too many passengers or too much gear.

☐ Defective scuppers which allow water to run into the vessel.

☐ Defective or broken hatches, or hatches left open which allow water in.

☐ Open transoms, which put vessels at risk of sinking the moment they lose power and forward motion.

☐ Bad electrical wiring or faults due to poor maintenance.

☐ Outboard motor wells, because openings for control cables which are not sealed properly allow water to leak in.

☐ Leaks in the bellows or boots that run between the engine and the partially submerged drive to the propeller on inboard motor vessels, because these degrade and crack and allow water to leak in.

☐ Leaving the bung out: We've all done it.

≈   ≈   ≈

AUSTRALIAN CRICKETERS Andrew Symonds and Matthew Hayden had a brush with tragedy while on a fishing trip during a break between test matches in December 1999.

They were flipped out of their boat, and were not

wearing lifejackets. Symonds has since appeared in television advertisements encouraging boaties to ensure they carry and use safety equipment.

The pair left harbour in Brisbane before dawn and were heading through the South Passage for a bar crossing to the open sea.

Symonds tells what happened: 'We were headed for the Amity Point Bar. I was driving and was using our GPS to follow the "bread crumbs" — the foam trail out that we had followed over the past few days — and although it was getting light, my direction was out that day and by the time we got close to getting through the sand bar and out into the open sea, we were probably 50 metres off where we should have been.

'Big mistake. Out of nowhere, a set of three huge waves stood up right in front of us. I looked over at Haydos to see what he reckoned we should do. "Give it a gutful," was his advice, so I did, and managed to get airborne over the first wave, but we landed heavily and dunked the motor, snuffing it out.

'A second later, the next wave hit us and pushed us half side-on, filling the boat up to our thighs. We tried to re-start the engine but there was no spark so we did a quick check of the battery and fuel line to see if anything had come loose but there was nothing wrong as far as we could see.

'Anyway, we were now totally side–on to the third wave and it was fairly clear we were going for a dip.

'Although there was no time to get the life jackets, just as we were about the take the plunge over the side, Haydos coolly grabbed his sunnies and tucked them into his togs! Moments later the third big wave swamped us and our boat began to sink below the surface, ending up seconds later with only the nose showing.'

Hayden: 'It all happened so bloody quickly. We hit a wave, came back hard down on our stern and water punched its way up the exhaust manifold. We had no power, we were right in the impact position on the bar and we were just stranded.'

It took them more than an hour to swim to shore at Stradbroke Island, through what are known as shark–infested waters, battling currents, crashing waves and eventually, shock and exhaustion.

After the incident their Queensland Bulls team-mates dubbed Symonds as 'Skipper' and Hayden as 'Gilligan' for the remainder of the summer.

≈   ≈   ≈

NEITHER FAME AS a sportsman nor the superior fitness of top athletes is any guarantee of safety at sea.

In February 2009, four young stars of America's National Football League set out from Florida for a day's fishing in the Gulf of Mexico. Three died. The fourth has been haunted by the event and its aftermath, suffering mental torment. He has had difficulty sleeping asking: 'Why me?'

The four had played together at the University of South Florida. Kevin Schuyler, then 24, had graduated to become an offensive end for Tampa Bay and he and fellow former team–mates Marquis Cooper, 26, who was by then a linebacker for the Oakland Raiders, and the Detroit Lions defensive ends Corey Smith, 29, and Will Bleakley, 25, were holidaying during the off–season. They were well offshore when their anchor stuck fast.

Manoeuvring around and trying to tow it out did not work. The weather was deteriorating. They should have cut the rope.

They were side–on as a larger–than–usual swell lifted the eight–metre boat, then threw it sideways. Water rushed over the gunwales, rolling it.

The four had no time to radio for help. They clung to the upturned hull through that day and into the night, and all through the next day.

But by nightfall they were losing strength due to hypothermia and one by one, all but Schulyer let go and slipped away before the next dawn.

Rescuers, alerted because the friends had not returned at the allotted time, scoured hundreds of square kilometres of ocean before finding Schuyler still alive, 43 hours later.

He survived because he had been violently sea–sick on the boat and, suffering the shivers, had donned a fleece jacket while the others were dressed in T–shirts.

The warmth of the jacket saved him from death — but, confused about why he was the sole survivor, he was unable to return to his former life. He left the football team and went into hiding, emerging more than a year later after writing a book about the tragedy.

'I think about it all the time,' he said then.

'The hardest time is at night when you are left without answers — I still ask myself every day "Why me?" I toss and turn at night and the mind's weak — you get started thinking about everything that happened, but especially "Why me?"'

≈   ≈   ≈

THE RULES REGARDING survival after a boat capsizes are universally known after the inquiries that follow deaths on the water. Yet people, including the experts, continue to ignore such standards as 'stay with the boat' and 'wear a lifejacket'.

In July 2010, a Royal Canadian Mounted Police boat with two Mounties aboard collapsed on the Stewart River in the Yukon.

Witnesses watched as one Mountie clung to the near–submerged boat as it floated downstream, while the other struck out for shore. Constable Michael Pavin, 26, didn't make it and was lost from sight.

Two of those on shore paddled a canoe out and rescued the other officer. Pavin 'was not wearing a personal floatation device,' the RCMP said.

≈   ≈   ≈

THE MOVIE *POSEIDON* which showed a cruise ship being upturned by a freak wave and the passengers' subsequent struggle for survival was etched in the public consciousness in the same way that *Jaws* made everyone scared of sharks.

But could such a thing happen?

Probably, because some huge ships have come close to roll–over. Modern cruise liners, however, have in–built stability systems which can return them to upright after a roll of up to 45 degrees.

Sinkings

Australians and New Zealanders were among the passengers injured when the Brisbane–based *Pacific Sun* rolled by around half that. The ship was hit by freak weather 600kms north of New Zealand. Of the 1,731 passengers and 671 crew, 77 were injured, some sustaining fractures.

The 223–metre, 47,000–tonne 10–deck liner was heading to Auckland from Port Vila, Vanuatu, when the weather deteriorated rapidly as people were sitting down to dinner.

The captain decided to change course to limit the roll in seven–metre seas but as he brought the ship around, it was pushed broadside–on to the seas and rolled at least 20 degrees.

Terrified passengers described the scene as 'like something out of a disaster movie' as chairs and other loose objects crashed around them. A bank of gaming machines was ripped from a bracket in the ship's casino, and the grand piano crashed across the ballroom. The degree of roll meant the spa and swimming pools were emptied of water, which flooded around the decks.

The ship docked safely two days later, and the P&O company offered passengers a 25% discount on the cost of a future cruise, but many swore they'd never put to sea again. P&O said the situation was 'exceptional, extremely unlikely ever to be repeated.'

In November 2010, a nine–metre wave hit the Maltese–flagged and Cypriot–owned cruise ship *Louis Majesty* as it was steaming in the Mediterranean, off Spain's Catalonia region. In gale force winds and rough seas, the 200–metre long *Louis Majesty* was hit head–on by three consecutive 'freak waves', the second and third of which smashed through the forward lounge windows.

Two people were killed by flying glass. Many others were injured by furniture and fittings being thrown around, or from being hurled across the ship as it rocked violently back and forth. The vessel was on the way to Genoa in Italy but had to dock at Barcelona for repairs and to disembark all passengers.

Those on board the United States–owned *Carnival Splendour* in November 2010 would have loved to have disembarked but were stuck for a week after fire destroyed electrical generators and disabled the ship on day one of a seven–day cruise off Mexico.

The ship was more than 200 miles from the US when the early–morning fire brought it to a halt. Because of the lack of electricity, there was no communication except the captain's back–up battery set. The ship had no cell phone connections, no refrigeration and so all the food spoiled. Passengers were deprived of air conditioning and hot showers.

By day four, the US Navy aircraft carrier which had been diverted to help was sending its helicopters to the *Carnival Splendour* with tins of spam and crab meat.

Tugboats sailed from Mexico and towed the ship to Ensenada from where the passengers were taken by bus back across the border, while the ship was towed for another three days to make San Diego Harbour.

The last major cruise liner sinking was in 2007 when a ship with more than 1,500 people on board went down after hitting rocks near the Aegean island of Santorini. Two French tourists died.

≈   ≈   ≈

NEW ZEALAND HAS had its own cruise liner disaster. The *Mikhael Lermantov* was a regular on the Australia–New Zealand–Pacific Island run, catering mainly to elderly tourists.

The 200–metre ship was built in East Germany in 1972, named after the 'poet of the Caucasus', and was owned by the Baltic Shipping Company, effectively the Soviet Union Government.

That became a major complication when she hit rocks in the Marlborough Sounds on February 16, 1986. She had left Picton Harbour in the afternoon and was to cruise in the Sounds.

At the wheel was the Picton pilot and harbourmaster, Captain Don Jamison. He wanted to show the elderly Australians aboard some good views and so travelled close to shore, near the appropriately named, as it turned out, Port Gore.

Captain Jamison made the poor decision to pass between rocks at the Cape Jackson passage. It was an area he knew well.

But on this day there was not sufficient water beneath the keel of the *Mikhael Lermantov* which had a draft of 5.5 metres.

At 5.37pm, and while travelling at 15 knots, the starboard side was ripped open on rocks. Jamison beached her but because the incoming water had flooded the engine room there was no power to lower the anchors and she drifted out to deep water again.

Nearby fishing and work boats could see her listing badly but all offers of help were refused.

Maritime Radio calls to the ship were rebuffed with the reply that everything was fine. The captain and crew were terrified of the implications of losing the vessel. No distress call was ever sent.

It was not until 8.30pm that people began to evacuate of their own accord. And it was not until nearly 10pm that formal evacuation was ordered.

The 740 on board were removed safely thanks to a

fleet of rescue boats that included the coastal tanker *MV Tarihiko* and the interisland ferry *Arahura*. One crewman, Pavel Zagladimov, died.

The ship sank in 38 metres of water and remains one of the most accessible dives to a large cruise ship anywhere in the world. Three people have died while diving on the wreck.

Captain Jamison cited the mental fatigue of consecutive 80–hour work weeks for his mistake. He resigned his post.

The Marlborough Harbour Board that employed him made an out–of–court compensation settlement with the Baltic Shipping Co.

≈   ≈   ≈

THE *CELTIC KIWI* was past its use–by date when it sank in October 1991 near North Cape while headed for Samoa with a load of cement.

My old mate Bruce 'Dilly' Dillner was aboard and I lost $100 as a result.

Dillner was a hardened seaman who had worked on fishing boats, delivered yachts overseas and crewed on cargo vessels. But he's one of those blokes who seem to have a storm cloud of trouble over them almost all the time. He's no longer at sea, having lost a middle finger and both legs in various accidents.

One day I was at work as a reporter at the *NZ Herald* and heard the emergency services scanner come alive with discussion about a seaman on a fishing vessel moored in the Viaduct Harbour in Auckland who had a badly broken leg.

The Fire Service had to be called to raise a stretcher on which he was lying from the boat deck to the wharf. It turned out he'd left the fishing boat at high tide, when its deck was near–level with the wharf.

He returned six hours later the worse for wear and jumped from the wharf to the deck, by now three metres below. His leg splintered in a compound fracture.

He went to bed, consoled with the bottle of spirits he'd carried home from the bar. Twelve hours later, tide–in and tide–out again, he woke in pain and called for help.

Not too long after this incident, Bruce came to see me while I was working at the *NZ Herald*, having just started my shift from 1pm–11pm. He needed $100 to get his passport back from hock so he could take up a job on the *Celtic Kiwi* which was leaving Auckland that evening.

Peter Barrowclough, then the owner of the Shakespeare Hotel, had fronted the money to him and kept the passport as security. Bruce came into the *Herald* for a subsidised cafeteria lunch.

I loaned him the money, he retrieved his travel document and then left town, promising I'd be repaid within a couple of weeks.

I went back to work and about six hours later, was sitting at the *Herald* desk ticking off minutes until knock–off time when a mayday distress call came across the emergency services scanner.

Sure enough, it was the *Celtic Kiwi*. She'd sprung plates as she hit the rough waters rounding the tip of New Zealand where the Tasman Sea and Pacific Ocean collide.

An inquiry found that the ship — formerly the *Holmdale* which had long worked the Chatham Islands run — suffered a major rupture to plates in the forward hold and suggested the weight she was carrying was possibly too much for her 30–year–old hull.

There could hardly be a more apt situation to explain the idiom 'she went down like a stone.'

The crew were immediately rescued by another journalist mate of mine, yachtsman Steve Raea, who was cruising back from the Pacific on his boat *Rock Steady*.

I told the boss at the *Herald* that I was assured of

a good rescue story and he dispatched myself and a cameraman to Opua where the yacht was to berth with the survivors.

When we got there, however, Raea circled his craft under motor just off the wharf for a few minutes. When they tied up, I was told in no uncertain terms that the *Herald* wouldn't be getting any information.

Unknown to me, Raea had just signed a deal to work for the Wellington paper *The Dominion* and, as rescuer, he wanted exclusive rights to impress his new boss.

'Dilly' had been sworn to secrecy. I couldn't blame him for that but I'm still waiting for my $100.

Eventually, 'Dilly' decided to work ashore. Things didn't change much for him. His first foray into attempting to run a fishing company resulted in a partnership with a lawyer and an accountant — he was the seafaring expert and the other two were supposed to handle the management.

Bruce admitted to surprise when just a few weeks later the managers instructed him to drive out to the Manukau office of the Inland Revenue Department to collect a cheque for around $500,000 that was owed to the company.

'Dilly' had family at Totara North on the northern side of the Whangaroa Harbour. The lawyer and accountant had sweetened his deal and bought a 'no questions' approach by leasing a brand new Holden for him and he was planning a weekend trip to Northland in it when we met for a beer after his visit to IRD on the Friday afternoon. He shouted, told me he'd done his first big deal.

Later, it turned out that the cheque from IRD was a refund of the Goods & Services Tax (GST) — the company had apparently and unknown to him purchased a fishing vessel named *The Reward* for $5 million and the $500,000 was an instant return on the GST paid.

It turned out that *The Reward* was a near–unserviceable derelict worth more like the GST return amount than the stated purchase price. The case became a forerunner for many subsequent GST fraud cases, the lawyer and accountant charged and 'Dilly' subpoenaed to give evidence against them.

'I couldn't believe they had a teenager signing a cheque for half a million dollars,' he confided to me later.

≈   ≈   ≈

Boaties' Tales

Wild harbours

'The westerly wind asserting his sway from the south–west quarter is like a monarch gone mad, driving forth with wild imprecations the most faithful of his courtiers to shipwreck, disaster and death.'
— English author Joseph Conrad (1857–1924).

The Manukau Harbour on the west coast of Auckland has a fearsome reputation, many souls having departed this world in the waters of its bar crossing.

This record stretches from the days of sailing ships including *Orpheus* in the 1800s through to January, 2010 when a five–metre runabout was rolled while trying to back out of an intended bar crossing, and a prison officer on board was killed.

In September 2010, the coastal freighter *Spirit*

of Resolution grounded on the harbour's shifting sandbanks. It is undoubtedly a place where care needs to be taken, where foolishness, inexperience or alcohol –fuelled sailors will quite probably find trouble.

It is also a very productive harbour and the waters just outside the heads and up the coast towards the deepwater Kaipara Trench hold everything from marlin and mahimahi to hapuku and bass, as well as giant snapper and kingfish, oversize Kermadec kahawai and the biggest gurnard you'll find anywhere.

The key is preparation, going when easterly winds have flattened the swell or at least straightened it out and smoothed the waters, and learning to read the waves.

The bar is constantly changing. The west coast sand is black because it is the breakdown of iron–laden volcanic rock from Taranaki, carried north by the prevailing current. The Tasman Sea produces wind–driven rollers of five metres and more.

The prevailing south–westerly wind turns this to mush. The mouth of this massive harbour is just 1,800 metres wide, from the tip of the Awhitu Peninsula to Paratutai Island, from where the kauri carriers once took timber shipments to London and San Francisco. Of the 394s/kms of harbour, nearly a third is exposed at low tide.

Tidal variation low–to–high can be as much as four metres.

Combine all these conditions and you end up with what the locals call 'the washing machine' at the harbour mouth; breaking rollers with white–tops of a metre or more, coming at you from four directions – swell–driven, wind–driven, tidal–driven and those rebounding off the sandbars and sharp cliffs that drop to the entrance.

The English first came to this area in numbers in the early 1800s to mill kauri because its straight bole, few substantial branches or knots, ability to flex and easy woodworking meant great timber for masts and hulls.

Later, this area and the Coromandel peninsula were plundered for timber to be milled into weatherboards sent to help rebuild San Francisco after the great earthquake and fire of 1906, where more than 3,000 were killed and 300,000 of the city's 410,000 were made homeless. Many of the old villas seen in television cop shows, in which criminals are chased down sloping streets towards the Golden Gate bridge, are made of New Zealand kauri.

The remains of railway tracks skirt Paratutai Rock. They run north to Karekare but most are now under metres of wind–driven black sand.

Onehunga was the centre of economic wealth for

the region, where sailing ships brought supplies from England and took back timber. A very large high-ceiling cave in the rock at the end of Whatipu Beach was turned into a ballroom, with a kauri floor laid. Families would make the boat trip from Onehunga and then take a horse-driven cart along the beach to grand balls, all dressed in their finery.

Cornwallis, just inside Puponga Point on the north side of the harbour, was designated by early city planners as Auckland's centre.

By the 1840s, they had reversed that decision and centred Auckland City on the Waitemata Harbour, despite forcing ships to take a longer route around North Cape. That diversion was simply because of the number of shipwrecks.

In 1908, the Government passed the Manukau Canal Act which allowed it to take land to connect the Manukau to the Waitemata, from Green Bay via the Whau Creek to Te Atatu. The Act remains in force today, the canal long forgotten.

Timber milling ceased around 1920. More recently, the boats shipwrecked have been smaller recreational vessels.

Close calls include the grounding of a Scandinavian explosives carrier that was expected to travel down the east coast to the ICI and army facility near Kawakawa

Bay. The captain thought there was a canal from the Manukau to the Waitemata.

The ship grounded, then luckily was lifted by a surging wave and thrown into deeper water and managed to push on to Onehunga. Unloaded, it still had to wait for a favourable tide that would ensure its bottom was clear of the seabed.

What a fireworks display that lot would have made had things gone differently!

Recent deaths include those of a crew member of the yacht *Tobamoray* in March 2005, when the vessel was swamped and sunk by a five-metre wave. An inquest found the boat had insufficient reserve buoyancy and that the buoyancy compartment allowed water in. Two crew survived.

On January 9, 2010, four mates headed towards the bar intending to make the crossing. The 'washing machine' was doing its thing and they decided to back out. But they did it the wrong way.

The boat flipped at about 8am but the coastguard were not notified until about 3.40pm, when someone on shore spotted the upturned hull.

Coastguard search and rescue co-ordinator John Cowan said the men did not notify the organisation they were about to cross the bar. They did not have waterproof communications equipment aboard and were unable to call for assistance. One of their mistakes was to try and turn in the 'washing machine'. The wave and wind action creates foam and air bubbles near the surface, which results in propellers not being able to grab the water, or cavitation.

Once you make the decision to go over the bar it definitely pays to carry on straight into the swell; if it's dodgy, go out and turn back in running straight with the swell. Another common mistake is on the return when skippers throttle their boats to sit in the trough between waves. There is more control, and more time to rectify any problems, if boats are sitting right on the backside of a forward–travelling wave.

That allows choice of a good time to scoot forward over the wave once the whitewash has subsided.

Manukau Coastguard president Peter Van Rooyen said his service gets between 20 and 30 call–outs a year, with about 120 people helped or rescued.

The number of incidents peaked in the mid–2000s when the coastguard was called out an average of 120 times a year.

'The fall in incidents must be attributed to the educational programs provided by coastguard and the fact that there seems to be a tendency for people to take better care and maintenance of their boats now,' Van Rooyen said.

Wild harbours

'The majority of the incidents inside the harbour, probably 80%, would be simple breakdowns that are electrical, mechanical or fuel–related. About 10% involve assisting the NZ Police with shoreline searches. The remaining 10% are callouts to incidents over the bar, many of which are also mainly electrical, mechanical etc. Most are caused through negligence and lack of knowledge.'

He is rightly proud of the organisation's rapid response times and its outstanding record for successful rescues without fatalities.

≈   ≈   ≈

MANUKAU COASTGUARD have had their own dramas on the bar. In 2010, a training exercise left one member with a broken leg and another suffering concussion when their rigid–hull inflatable was twice pitched from the top of waves estimated at five metres.

Van Rooyen explains: 'Due to the nature of the seas coastguard are expected to go out in, to effect a rescue in some cases on the west coast of New Zealand, our training regime includes going out on the Manukau Bar in some adverse conditions. Although all safety precautions and protocol are adhered to, it is the nature of the sea that it is unpredictable. If coastguard did not train in adverse conditions then they would be ineffective in a rescue in poor conditions.'

There are simple warnings.

'Some of the vessels we have towed would be better used for firewood rather than fishing, but unfortunately with the present economic environment we do see a small portion of vessels that have had no maintenance done on them, the motors are not serviced by a licensed service agent and the vessels themselves are in a poor state.'

The Manukau, Papakura and Waiuku Coastguard groups combine to hold a Bar Crossing Awareness Day twice a year, to instruct and inform members of the public who intend crossing the Bar on the dangers and what to look for.

Important procedures a boatie needs to follow before crossing a bar include: check the weather, check the swell height. Tell someone what your intentions are.

Most importantly, file a trip report with the coastguard at frequency '22' or the general coastguard channel '16' on the VHF band. They like to know when you are about to leave harbour, to hear again when you have successfully completed the crossing, and vice–versa on the way home.

'Make sure you are on the correct radio channel and

most importantly of all wear a life jacket. If you have a hand held VHF, strap it to your arm. If you can afford a personal EPIRB, all the better,' Van Rooyen said.

The coastguard does not advise use of the northern channel, which has closed down to within a few metres in some places and, in wind–against–tide situations can be extremely ugly.

The south channel is known to move widely after the regular storms that lash the west coast.

For a first–time bar crossing you cannot beat local knowledge and it is wise to either let a local drive your boat or at least to follow one out the channel.

Just remember Rule Number One: 'If In Doubt, Don't Go Out.'

≈   ≈   ≈

THE ENTRANCE TO the Kaipara Harbour is rightly labelled 'The Graveyard'.

By 2011, 113 shipwrecks had been officially-recorded and some historians suggest as many as 30 more have gone unrecorded.

The harbour covers an area of 947 square kilometres, meaning it is the largest by area in the world. At low tide, 409 square kilometres of this area is out of the water.

About 1,190 million cubic metres of water goes in or out at each tide and the current can reach five knots or 9km/h at peak flow as it heads towards the narrow entrance.

This current also shifts around the black sand that flows up the coast from Taranaki and the Waikato River. The constantly changing sandbars, the force of the current, high winds and big swells have come together in various combinations to bring about the undoing of many a sailor.

Maori say the chief Rongomai was drowned on the Kaipara bar when his ocean–going canoe *Mahuhu* was overturned in the surf.

The first recorded European shipwreck was of the 550–tonne barque *Aurora* in 1840. She had landed English settlers at Te Kopuru and was returning to England with kauri spars when she was swamped on the bar. She was eventually refloated and repaired.

Many others were not so lucky.

The *Sophia Pate* was lost in 1841. The *Mary Catherine*, also carrying kauri, was anchored inside the harbour in preparation to leave when she was lost.

The incoming spring tide was so strong it broke her mooring chains and she was pushed side–on onto a sandbar and rolled.

In those days, professional salvagers lived in the area

because they could make good money retrieving what they could, by boat and by using grappling hooks to troll the sandbars. Many artefacts are in museums around the Northland coast. The Dargaville Museum features the frontal figurehead of the *Lady St Aubyn* which was wrecked in 1851.

The *Mosquito*, owned by a French Count, was lost never to be seen again.

The locals tell of ship remains that appear one day and disappear the next, both off the coast and in the sand dunes behind the beach, as tidal currents and strong winds shift sand around. The dunes average 30 metres in height and the tallest is 60 metres.

One of the more unusual claims is that locals found and dived on a German U–boat. The story had it that the submarine came to the Northland coast in late 1944 to drop off 13 high–ranking Nazis who realised that Germany was going to lose World War Two and it was said they brought looted treasures with them to finance a new start in life. No proof has ever been presented and the existence of the U–boat wreck has never been verified.

A lighthouse was built at Poutu Point in 1884 to help ships through the treacherous passage. But within 30 or so years, the kauri rush was over and no more large vessels crossed the bar. Instead, cargo was taken to Auckland through the Waitemata Harbour on the east coast.

The last recorded wreck in 'The Graveyard' was of the yacht *Aosky* in 1994.

Kaipara's status as the world's largest harbour puts it ahead of some of the most–used harbours in the world, many of which also lay claim to the title of the 'world's largest harbour'.

Contenders include Port Jackson (Sydney Harbour), Cork in Ireland, Poole in Dorset in south England, Nova Scotia in Canada and Trincomalee in Sri Lanka.

Sydney is undoubtedly the world's largest navigable harbour but at 55 square kilometres it is a tiddler in terms of overall size when compared to Kaipara (947 square kilometres) and Manukau (394 square kilometres).

Poole is 48 square kilometres but its average depth at high tide is only 48 centimetres and it has just one navigable channel.

Trincomalee is slightly smaller again, in fifth place, and is followed by Nova Scotia and Cork.

≈   ≈   ≈

Aground

'Only two sailors, in my experience, never ran aground. One never left port and the other was an atrocious liar.'
— *Don Bamford, Canadian seafarer and author.*

It is easy to run aground in both the Manukau and Kaipara Harbours. I've done it on both. On dim days in winter, the sea and sky can morph into the same dull, featureless grey colour.

I was a passenger in a four–metre runabout speeding across the Kaipara one such day when we ran slap–bang into a sandbar just centimetres below the surface.

The water was flat calm and there was not a sign of a ripple or current to indicate the lack of depth. The boat stopped dead, the motor chewing in sand. I was holding the plexiglass windscreen and on impact took it with me straight over the bow and into the shallow water. The skipper smacked his head on the wheel.

The tide was falling and it took us more than 30 minutes with me walking the boat before we found navigable water again.

On the Manukau, we make use of such sandbars to gather scallops on spring low tides, when you can get a limit bag of 20 in half that number of minutes in ankle–deep water.

But the bars shift. On one such venture we set the GPS for the last–known position of the scallop bar we had worked about a month prior. Since then, the harbour had been reshaped by big storms, major runoff from land, high winds and swell.

And so it was that as we were powering down in preparation to look for the bar, it found us.

It was an inopportune place to hit ground, one of the few where there is some solid rock structure. The hull showed a bad split and was leaking water.

It was slack water so we got our scallops. But when we looked in the boat, which had been held by anchor for about 10 minutes, the floor was full of water and it was rising as the hull settled deeper.

We jumped aboard and headed for shore, and it immediately became apparent there was an optimum speed at which we should travel; not too fast nor too slow, both of which caused a leak like a stream from a fire hose. With bilge pumps and buckets going full bore, we were lucky.

≈   ≈   ≈

THE NAME *TIRI* became synonymous with Radio Hauraki in the latter half of the 1960s and the early 1970s as the group of mates led by David Gapes took to the seas to challenge government opposition to private radio.

They were driven by the idea of giving listeners what they were not getting from State–controlled radio, and that was rock 'n' roll.

Journalist Gapes, ad–man Derek Lowe and New Zealand Broadcasting Corporation announcer Chris Parkinson launched Hauraki, named after Auckland's Hauraki Gulf, in 1966. Their idea was borrowed from England where so–called radio pirates had sailed beyond the then three–mile offshore limit so they could broadcast signals into England without being subject to that country's broadcasting laws, regulations and financial charges. Those pirates inspired the 2009 film *The Boat That Rocked* starring Kiwi Rhys Darby.

Authorities in Wellington were determined to stop the Hauraki rebellion. As *Tiri* left her mooring in Auckland's Viaduct Basin in October 1966, Radio

Hauraki had mustered hundreds of supporters to see her off. Police were there in numbers. They ordered Auckland Harbour Board staff to close the drawbridge that opened to the Waitemata Harbour.

Two Hauraki supporters ran and squatted in the steel jaws of the pivot mechanism of the bridge so it could not be closed.

Tiri moved on, but the ship's main mast got caught in the partially lowered drawbridge. A rope was run ashore and members of the crowd helped to haul the ship free.

As it passed the bridge, the police launch *Deodar* ran across her bow; the cops boarded *Tiri* and shut down her engines.

The crew were arrested and as they were taken off the *Tiri* they sang the Beatles song *We All Live In A Yellow Submarine.*

Eleven people were charged with obstructing a Marine Department inspector but the charges were dropped soon after, and the *Tiri*, which had been towed to the Devonport Naval Base, was returned to the owners.

By 1968, pirate radio was established in Auckland, with Hauraki selling lots of advertising because it was widely supported by the public for its music as well as its anti—authoritarian stance.

Aground

But on January 28, 1968, disaster struck when the *Tiri* suffered engine failure while seeking shelter from a storm at Whangaparapara Harbour on Great Barrier Island. She was blown onto rocks.

Listeners heard the on–air announcer describe the grounding and his final broadcast before he abandoned ship. He told listeners: 'Hauraki News — Hauraki crew is abandoning ship. This is Paul Lineham aboard the *Tiri*. Good night.'

His words were followed by a station jingle, and then the sound of the ship's hull striking the rocks.

The broadcasting equipment was salvaged but the boat was a wreck. Four days later, the pirates bought the boat *Kapuni* and renamed her *Tiri II*.

Tiri II was blown from her mooring at Great Barrier on April 3 that year and was nearly lost at sea. And in June, she was blown onto the beach at Uretiti, south of Whangarei, and had to be towed free.

Hauraki had been broadcasting at sea for 1,111 days when in March 1970, the National Government finally bowed to public pressure and granted Radio Hauraki the first private broadcasting licence in New Zealand.

The pirates steamed for Auckland in jubilant mood but this was broken when announcer Rick Grant fell overboard and drowned near Channel Island at the tip of the Coromandel Peninsula.

GEOFF LAMOND SPENT four years at university studying agribusiness and at the end of his studies, he had learned one major thing — 'I realised it was the last thing I wanted to do for the rest of my life.'

He had paid his way through 'varsity by working on charter boats and so he headed in that direction for more work, serving an apprenticeship with well-regarded charter skippers John Baker on *Ma Cherie* and Rick Pollock on *Pursuit*, and he hasn't looked back. He became a partner in the chartering business using the 47-foot *Aranui*, a sleek and well-appointed vessel built by O'Brien Boats in Townsville, North Queensland, working out of Auckland in the winter and then fishing the Three Kings Islands and other northern parts from January to June.

In mid-April, 2007, he was skippering the boat *Outer Limits*, working out of Houhora. It was about 8pm, they had just finished a charter and were readying the boat for the next day. They were looking forward to a good night's sleep in harbour when a distress call came over the VHF radio.

Pollock's boat *Pursuit* had been blown onto a rock ledge about 300 metres from the beach behind Murimotu Island, right on North Cape. Lamond waited to hear if a closer boat could respond but when it quickly became apparent there wasn't one, Lamond and crew left Houhora into a building swell and wind blowing up from the south.

'I'd just finished an oil change and didn't have time to check things,' he recalled.

It was more than two hours to the Cape in the following swell. When they got there they found *Pursuit* being rolled side–to–side and in danger of breaking up on a reef. The Northland rescue chopper had already over–flown the boat with the intention of taking the crew and clients off but decided it was too risky.

While Lamond stood *Outer Limits* bow into the swell and backed down on the ledge, his deckhands Chris Ash and James Brown brought a light line to the stern of *Pursuit* via rowboat, and a heavier tow rope was fed across.

I was on *Pursuit* that night. It was no fun.

We were at anchor in calm water after an evening's fishing for snapper. We were just about to eat dinner when a freak gust of wind akin to a mini–tornado swept around the headland, came from behind us and surfed the 17–metre vessel onto the rocks. Pollock started the engines and the second he put her in gear we all heard the two propellers shear off.

After hours unable to do anything but listen to the boat creaking and smashing, and fearing it would break up, we were ecstatic to see Lamond and his crew.

It's interesting how people react under pressure. One of the charter clients sat in *Pursuit*'s cabin reading a copy of *Penthouse*. At the other end of the anxiety scale was an older, experienced charter angler who was at near–panic, and talking about death and praying.

Outer Limits strained against the weight of *Pursuit* and it took several attempts before she finally broke free on a rising tide. They pulled us stern–first to sea until we were far enough from land to change the tow line to the bow.

We then faced many hours of pitching, yawing and near–rolling as we were hauled back to Houhora.

The line broke three times, shattering forward hatches and portholes and smashing the front railing, each time leaving the boat in a frightening drift until re–attached and heading south again.

It was dawn as we pulled into a beautifully calm Houhora Harbour. As we sat around the table drinking coffee, Lamond's eyes were as red as I've ever seen anyone's, the concentration required to make the trip etched across his face. It was great seamanship, as was Pollock's under tow.

They're the sort of guys you can trust your life to — I know because I did.

'I'd have done it for anyone, it didn't make any

difference who was stuck there but knowing it was Rick, it made for an emotional night,' Lamond said of towing his old boss.

≈   ≈   ≈

RESIDENTS OF Mt Maunganui woke one morning in late 2010 to find the launch *Paradise* beached in their swimming spot next to Marine Parade.

It could not be re–floated before major damage was caused. A navigational error had brought about a $650,000 loss.

The skipper, Daryl Hodson, then 47, was spending six months of the year managing a resort in Fiji with his wife and the other six months flying helicopters in the South Island. He bought the boat in 2002 and had taken it to Fiji, the Marshall Islands and American Samoa.

Hodson, his 75–year–old father and a friend, had travelled from Fiji, cleared Customs at Opua the day before and were intending to head into Tauranga Harbour. At 10.30pm on October 20, 2010, the coastguard received a mayday call to assist. The 16–metre launch had been driven straight into rocks at Rabbit Island, tearing a 1.5–metre hole in the front of the hull.

Hodson said afterwards he didn't remember much about the collision itself and believed he must have fallen asleep at the wheel. He couldn't understand how he had drifted off after having a refreshing shower and dinner at 8pm.

'I got knocked out of the helm chair and down through the internal access, and I was knocked unconscious,' he said.

His friend realised the boat was taking on water and so they launched their dinghy and sent the distress call. Hodson recovered and turned the boat towards the beach so it didn't sink in deep water.

The mayday call brought a quick response from a tugboat that was engaged in guiding a container ship into Tauranga but by the time it arrived at the scene, his father and their friend were already in the dinghy headed to shore and the *Paradise* was aground 100 metres from Marine Parade.

Its fuel tanks contained 600 litres of diesel and the launch carried 600 litres more stored in containers.

Hodson said his main concern was the environmental impact the wreck might have caused. But he had no control over the salvage operation.

Salvage rights to the uninsured launch were sold and attempts made to refloat her by pulling her back off the beach. By then, wet sand was acting like a suction cup on the hull and *Paradise* wouldn't budge.

A crane was brought in and strops tied around the hull to try and lift her up the beach. In the end, the transom ripped out and the starboard side collapsed.

Hodson wanted flotation bags put around the hull and an attempt made to float the launch to Bridge Marina but that never happened.

While watching *Paradise* being dismantled by a digger so it could be removed from the beach in parts, he described the salvage attempt as 'a fiasco, it's an absolute circus. They've trashed it. I had no say in the matter. I can't believe how they've gone about this.'

≈   ≈   ≈

Boaties' Tales

Small boats

'There is NOTHING— absolutely nothing — so much worth doing as messing about in boats.'
— *Kenneth Graham from* The Wind In the Willows.

Yachties on the open ocean have three major fears — fire, losing the bottom of their boat by hitting a whale or a half-sunk container, and being run down by mega-carrier container ships.

Their fears are justified as these are the three major causes of yachties drowning, well ahead of storm sinkings and man-overboard incidents.

Once fire takes hold, it generally can't be stopped and boats well alight tend to burn to the waterline. Even expert sailors can hit whales. Researchers for the American National Atmospheric and Oceanic Administration, who were studying the endangered North Atlantic whale, slammed into one with the propeller of their boat badly raking its back.

Whales tend to feed on plankton just below the surface and can be impossible to spot.

Steve Lassley from San Diego was fishing for marlin out of Cabo San Lucas in Mexico aboard his game boat when he rammed a whale at 22 knots. It split the boat's hull but he managed to limp back to port.

'I don't know how the boat stayed afloat,' he said.

A couple sailing off Cape Town, South Africa, were stunned when they saw a pod of whales surfacing about 200 metres from their 10–metre yacht. They believed the mammals were going to pass under their boat but one launched itself from the water right next to the yacht and crashed down on the deck, snapping the mast.

Chunks of blubber were left on the deck when the animal slid back into the water. Another yacht was nearby and video footage its crew took of that incident can be seen on *YouTube*.

Englishman Valentine Picton was fortunate the sea was flat calm when his launch *Ocean Land* motored into a whale off Cape Brett in the Bay of Islands in January 2006.

Picton, his wife and their five children were planning to cruise the Northland coast after staying the night at Paihia. He had seen a whale while heading along the coast at 7.30am, and steered away from it before feeling a 'thud' that lifted the boat. The engine room quickly filled with water and the launch sank within minutes. The family took to their dinghy and were quickly rescued.

In November 1995, a North American family, the Sleavins, were sailing down the north–east coast of New Zealand, towards the Bay of Islands late one night, when their yacht was run down by the Korean container ship *Pan Grace*.

The *Pan Grace* turned around, which took some miles and more than 20 minutes, and found Mrs Judith Sleavin afloat and rescued her.

Her husband and two children were dead.

≈   ≈   ≈

ON NUMEROUS occasions, large cargo ships have hit yachts and have continued on their way.

The round–the–world yachtie, Jessica Watson, was sailing her 10.4–metre yacht *Pink Lady* in a shipping lane off Stradbroke Island, near Brisbane, when the Chinese–owned tanker *Silver Yang* barged into her at 2.30am, breaking the mast and snapping rigging. Crew turned off its radar so it couldn't be tracked and it steamed to Hong Kong, where the captain and crew faced interrogation.

Five friends sailing from Cherbourg in France to Hamble in England in 2010 were left in the water when their yacht was sunk by a container ship that did not stop. The collision happened in heavy fog in the English Channel. The friends' mayday call was heard and they were rescued by the ferry *Condor Express*.

Low cloud and rain heralded an approaching storm off Cape Hatteras in the United States when the Swedish yacht *Mea* was hit by an unidentified tanker.

The collision ripped a three–metre gash down the side of *Mea* and the two people on board took to their liferaft. They fired off several flares, one of which was spotted by the master of the cargo ship *Star of Ismene*, which picked them up 80 nautical miles off shore.

The *Star of Ismene* was a regular on the Singapore–New York run and her usual course was further out to sea where the flares would not have been spotted, but on this occasion it was running closer to land to skirt the storm.

Four mates were aboard the yacht *Debonair,* moored in Dublin Harbour to watch a St Patrick's Day fireworks display in 2009, when they were run down by the grain carrier *Bluebird*. Three were killed.

The racer *Mureadrittas XL* was competing in a transatlantic run and was leading the race when it hit a stray container and was quickly sunk. The crew of three men and one woman got off a mayday call and took to their liferaft 600 nautical miles off Hawaii. A US Air Force Hercules dropped food supplies to them because they were far from shipping lanes and had to wait a day for rescue.

Yachties claim there are probably thousands of containers floating just below the surface of the world's oceans, half-sunk by their weight but held in suspension just out of sight due to air pockets and insulation.

When yachts simply vanish off the face of the earth, container collision is the oft-offered explanation.

≈   ≈   ≈

MUTINY ON THE high seas is legally defined as concerted disobedient or seditious action by two or more persons in military or naval service, or by sailors on commercial vessels.

Mutiny may range from a combined refusal to obey orders, to active revolt or going over to the enemy. Sailing can become a torturous experience when crew are at loggerheads.

Two novice sailors sparked a rescue after a bizarre 'mutiny' while on their first-ever yacht trip. Spike

Sellers, 34, bought the 12–metre yacht *Argo* in Cyprus in early 2010 and was sailing it home to Fort William, Scotland. He had invited his best friend, Ivan Holroyd, 34, and Holroyd's girlfriend, Rachel Rosen, 32, on the trip.

They hit heavy weather off the coast of Spain. Holroyd and Rosen wanted to turn back and head for port.

Sellers refused. The weather and seas worsened and they wanted to call for rescue. He stopped them doing so. So they jumped him and sat on him while they tied him up and then made the emergency call.

A rescue helicopter flew to the boat and plucked off Holroyd and Rosen.

Sellers refused to abandon his yacht and the chopper had to leave. Another was sent out and naval crew boarded the yacht and lifted Sellers off.

Because of the considerable expense, the trio were arrested on warrant and appeared in a Spanish court, where Judge Natalia Canosa investigated and decided Holroyd and Rosen would not face any charges and nor would Sellers.

The *Argo* was towed to land by a salvage company engaged by Sellers but he had no money to pay and had to stay in the northern Spanish port of Carino, trying to raise the $6,000 fee before the company would return the boat to him. He asked the couple for financial help but it was not forthcoming.

'They want to have nothing more to do with him. They just want to get back home as soon as they can and they'll be flying,' a friend of the couple said.

'Sailing will be out of the question for a long time to come.'

≈   ≈   ≈

MUTINY BROUGHT a 27–year friendship to an abrupt end in bad weather off the west coast of Northland.

Nelson accountant Bill Heritage invited his friends Carl Horn, John Lammin and Sharan Foga to sail with him from Auckland to Nelson in his 7.9–metre Compass 790 yacht named *Air Apparent,* and they set off in early March 2008.

They were hit by severe north–easterly gales after rounding Cape Reinga, and the crew insisted Heritage call for rescue as they believed the yacht was going to sink.

The Northland Emergency Services helicopter flew from Whangarei and lifted all four off the yacht, though Heritage told them he wanted to stay on board.

When they were landed, wrapped in blankets and

soaking wet, the skipper was not talking to the crew and vice–versa. Intermediaries told the crew that Heritage regarded them as responsible for the loss of his $24,000 craft and that he would be pursuing them for the money. The trio flat refused to pay.

At the time, a rescue helicopter pilot said that with good seamanship, the yacht could have easily ridden out the conditions.

Heritage maintained the boat was never in danger. The crew said it was ill–prepared for the west coast seas.

Horn said the motor would not work because the batteries were flat and the crank wouldn't start it. As a result of the loss of power, they had no navigation lights, no light on the compass and no communications. They wanted to deploy the sea anchor but it had no shackle and no rope attached.

They believed they would not have survived the night, Horn said. He denied any suggestion that the inexperienced crew panicked when the seas got rough and the wind reached 25 knots.

'The three of us put our trust in him. He was the sailor. We were crew, we were workers, we trusted implicitly in his skill.'

They hadn't slept for two days prior to making the rescue call and the three crew were becoming extremely uncomfortable with their situation as the gale increased, he said.

'I concluded that Bill had not prepared as well as he might have and that he was an optimist.'

Heritage was eventually paid out $23,000 by AMP Insurance which decided that 'mutiny was not reasonably foreseeable.'

Nearly nine months after being abandoned, the yacht was found south of Norfolk Island by French Navy patrol ship *La Moqueuse* which was on a trip from Noumea to Nelson. Its captain, Lieutenant Laurent Saunois, said the yacht was like a 'ghost ship'.

≈   ≈   ≈

A 'TRAINING CRUISE' turned into a bitter fall–out between novice sailors off the coast of Chile in January 2010.

Australian Mitchell Westlake and Canadians Jade Chabot and Lisa Hanlon paid $3,500 each for what was supposed to be a 40–day ocean sailing course aboard the 46 foot steel yacht *Columbia*, sailing from Salinas, Ecuador.

The yacht was owned and skippered by Boguslaw (Bob) Norwid, a Polish–born French citizen, and his wife. They were due to dock in Coquimbo, Chile, at the end of February. On the day they were expected in port, a massive earthquake registering 8.8 on the Richter scale struck Chile, triggering a tsunami.

Family of the trainees tried to contact them and, when not able to, they became concerned the boat had not arrived because of the tsunami.

They instigated a search campaign which included the rescue resources of five South American countries and every passenger ship cruising in the area.

The yacht arrived at its intended destination 35 days late, with those on board arguing bitterly.

It turned out they had been becalmed off the Chilean coast for a month. By then, the three trainees said they had one tin of tuna and one cup of rice per day to share between the three of them.

The yacht owners, the Norwids, had better food and more of it but they kept it in their cabin and would not share.

The crew wanted to use the radio to call for help, to arrange a food drop–off. Bob Norwid wouldn't let them, they said, saying it would drain the batteries.

So the crew went on strike, refusing to perform any work on the boat, and relations worsened.

Authorities in Ecuador interviewed Norwid for refusing his crew use of the ship's radio to let their families know they were safe. But he was allowed to sail away, as angry relatives of the crew threatened legal action.

≈ ≈ ≈

A KIWI WAS the first to sail solo through the famed Nor'West Passage.

Global warming helped, freeing the Arctic seas of ice so Aucklander Graeme Kendall could make the dangerous trip from the Atlantic Ocean, across the top of North America, to the Pacific.

The Passage was long-sought by sailing ships in the early days of ocean exploration and became something of an idyllic goal, as it cuts much time off the voyage from Europe to the Americas and vice-versa.

Some shipping made it but more was either lost, hemmed in or delayed by sea ice and as a result, the NW Passage route has never been widely used, always remaining on seafarers' wish-list.

Kendall first attempted the solo yacht trip through the 2,000 nautical mile Passage in 2005 but was blocked in by ice. He ran out of money and had to sell his boat, *Astral Express*.

The buyer, Edward Niclasen, from Greenland, kept in touch with Kendall and in 2010 loaned him the boat back so he could complete his dream. The trip took

12 days over the Arctic summer, ending September 9, and Kendall then sailed the *Astral Express* back to Auckland, arriving at the end of October.

'It was quite a risk,' Niclasen said. No insurance company was willing to provide cover for boat or skipper.

The pair remained in radio contact throughout. At the end of the pioneering trip, Kendall asked for just an apple and a beer.

'It's magic, just magic,' he said.

≈   ≈   ≈

WE WERE SAILING just off the Pittwater Harbour at the top of Sydney's Northern Beaches one day with a bunch of my wife's workmates, one of whom owned the yacht.

Another had the nickname 'Duck.' And so it came to changing tack and the skipper called out 'Duck' as the boom swung from port to starboard.

Duck stood up and said 'Yeah', and then was swept overboard by the boom.

≈   ≈   ≈

NORWEGIAN EXPLORER Thor Heyerdahl

crossed the Pacific on a wooden raft in 1947 with plaited bamboo as sails to back his theory that Polynesians had originated in South America.

The *Kon–Tiki* was named after the Incan Sun God. It was built in Peru from balsa logs 14 metres long that were lashed together with vines.

The raft was loaded with fresh water, coconuts, gourds, sweet potatoes and dried fish and vegetables.

Its crew were six Scandinavians who pushed off on an expedition that would last 101 days and end 6,500 kilometres away, at the uninhabited island of Raroia in the Taumotu Islands, near Tahiti.

Heyerdahl wrote a book about the experience and produced a movie of the expedition, which won an Academy Award in 1951.

But his theory has been widely discredited by anthropologists, who have better evidence to show that Polynesians are descended from Asians who used prevailing winds and currents to populate the Pacific whereas Heyerdahl's trip was against the weather patterns and therefore against the odds.

That didn't stop another Scandinavian expedition from recreating the trip.

In 2006, a crew including Heyerdahl's grandson, Olav, retraced the journey.

Boaties' Tales

Records

'The sea hates a coward.'
— Eugene O'Neill, American playwright (1888–
1953).

Attempting to set the world water speed record is a dangerous business. About 85% of those who have tried have died in the process.

The existing record was set by Australian Ken Warby, who recorded the mark of 511km/h (317mph) on Lake Blowering, near the town of Tumut in the Snowy Mountains of southern New South Wales, on October 8, 1978.

Records have been officially kept since 1928, the rule being that two consecutive passes must be made over the same piece of water and the speed recorded is the average of the two runs.

American brothers George and Gar Wood were the

early frontrunners, after both broke the 100mph mark, and George held it against his brother's attempts to pass him when he raised the mark to 149mph in his boat *Miss America VII* on the Detroit River in 1929.

In 1930, the British decided to have a crack and former race car driver Sir Henry Seagrave pushed the record to 158mph in *Miss England* at Windermere in the Lakes District. Having set the record, he tried to improve it with a third run and died in the attempt when he hit a log.

By 1932, Gar Wood had broken 200mph.

Five years later, the British mounted another record campaign with Malcolm Campbell as their driver and he reached 203mph and then 228mph after using a double–hulled hydroplane for the first time.

World War Two halted record attempts but post–war, the boats were driven by jet turbines rather than piston engines. In 1950, the Seattle car dealer Stanley Sayres took the record out to 260mph in his boat *Slo–Mo–Shun IV* and by 1952 he had improved this to 287mph.

In 1952, American John Cobb died after having reached 386mph when the front planing disc on his duel–hull racer collapsed and his boat bit into the water and broke up. In 1954, Italian Mario Verga died in similar fashion.

Records

The following year, Malcolm Campbell's son, Donald, pushed the record out to 325mph and over the following nine years he broke the record six times to set a new mark of 444mph.

In 1964, Campbell also set a new land speed record at 648km/h (403mph) on the dry bed of Lake Eyre in Western Australia. He remains the only man to hold both simultaneously.

By 1967, he had fitted a new Bristol–Siddeley Orpheus jet turbine which provided 4,500 pounds of thrust to *Blue Bird VII* and was aiming to break 300mph (480km/h). In his first run on Coniston Water, the largest lake in the Lakes District of Cumbria, he reached 297mph. His routine was to wait for refuelling before taking the return run.

But conditions looked like they might deteriorate so Campbell turned the boat around and powered up again.

He was doing 320mph and was 90% of the way down the measured kilometre distance when he hit a wake wave from his first run that raised the nose of *Blue Bird*.

Air got beneath the twin hulls and lifted her off the water and after catapulting she came down nose–first and disintegrated.

Pieces of the boat were recovered but Campbell's

body was not found until May 2001, 34 years after the accident.

In 1967, the Americans took the record back when Lee Taylor reached 459km/h in his boat *Hustler*.

Taylor died in 1980 while attempting to better Warby's record on Lake Tahoe. And Craig Arfors was killed in another attempt in 1989.

More than twenty years later, no one has tried to challenge the record again.

≈   ≈   ≈

AUCKLANDER Graeme Weller set a world record speed in the grand prix powerboat class when he drove his double–hill racer to 275.6km/h (172mph) on Lake Karapiro in the Waikato in October 2010.

The boat was powered by a turbo–charged 510 cubic inch Chevrolet V8 which produced 2000bhp.

≈   ≈   ≈

HIS MATES SAY Craig 'Ginger' Gibbs was destined for a life at sea.

Born in the lighthouse at the Mokohinau Islands in 1954, he ran away from home at 14 to join a ship as cabin boy.

Later, he fished out of Great Barrier. In the 1990s, he moved to the mainland where he set up the well-known waterfront restaurant and bar Swashbucklers and took up an interest in powerboat racing in the diesel–powered *Calico Jack*, setting records on the Manuwatu, Whanganui and Waikato Rivers.

In March 2006, Gibbs set the record for the fastest crossing of the Tasman Sea from Sydney Harbour Bridge to the Auckland Harbour Bridge. He used a high–powered rigid hull inflatable to beat the time of 47 hours 30 minutes set by the P&O liner *Oriana* in the 1970s. He and his three crew took 40 hours 31 minutes.

They refuelled halfway across, using a boat stationed for the purpose, and finding the mother ship when they had barely a cupful of petrol left in the tanks of the 12.5–metre Rayglass Protector.

≈   ≈   ≈

SOME ADVENTURERS are driven to push all boundaries and to sometimes go beyond reasonably acceptable and calculated risks, for reasons unfathomable to the rest of us.

Cross–Tasman kayaker Andrew McAuley was one such person.

At 39, McAuley had a young son, Finlay, four, and a loving wife Vicky when he made the ill-fated decision to try to become the first to paddle a kayak more than 2,000kms from Australia to New Zealand in 2007. He planned to paddle from Tasmania to the west coast of New Zealand's South Island.

As he departed on his journey, in his boat *First One,* Finlay ran along the beach shouting, 'Bye, Daddy.' His wife told television cameras: 'His fear-factor is zilch.'

But McAuley had his own camera recording his departure, and it revealed him in tears, saying, 'I'm very scared, I have a boy who needs a father and a wife who needs a husband.'

Mariners know the Tasman Sea as an extremely dangerous piece of water, and that it's used by the world's largest ships.

Storms spinning off Antarctica bring huge wind-driven swells. Passenger liners and their high-paying customers have been thrown around with major damage and injuries.

McAuley took his courage for the trip from his experience as an accomplished mountaineer, and he had previously paddled across the Gulf of Carpentaria in northern Australia in 2004 — a trip of 150kms on generally calm waters that took him 35 hours.

He had also paddled across Bass Strait from

Records

Melbourne to Tasmania, a journey that took 150 hours to cover 240kms. On that trip, he was near shipping lanes and always within reach of rescue.

Then he circled Antarctica, covering 800kms in eight weeks. He was named Australian Adventurer of the Year in 2006. But when he left Tasmania for New Zealand, he mis–read the weather.

After two days at sea, being battered by savage winds and high seas, he was forced to admit defeat and was suffering from hypothermia.

He made land at Maria Island, a sea–rise rock off Tasmania's east coast similar to Little Barrier in New Zealand — a nature reserve with sheer cliffs and few landing opportunities.

The Tasmanian Police delayed his second attempt at crossing the Tasman, demanding a kayak safety inspection. They wanted a demonstration of the craft's ability to right itself and to inspect safety and emergency gear before lifting a 'detention order' restraining him from departure.

The five–metre kayak had numerous in–built air-pockets to aid self–righting. He could sleep by setting a sea anchor to create drag, releasing his paddling seat and sliding down inside the kayak.

He then pulled over him a fibreglass canopy that slid forward from the rear of the kayak on rails, a cover he and his backers nicknamed 'Casper' because it looked like the head of Casper, the cartoon ghost.

McAuley said he could sleep 'like a mummy'. The kayak was designed to ride out severe storm conditions.

He left on January 11, 2007, and this time his departing words were more than prophetic.

'I hope I haven't bitten off more than I can chew.'

Not far out, he was shadowed for some time by a great white shark, which eventually lost interest. He paddled solidly, averaging 40kms a day, for 30 days.

But McAuley couldn't keep the kayak dry inside and he developed bad pressure and salt sores on his backside and elsewhere, plus he couldn't keep warm. He had to take sleeping pills to rest and regain strength.

At one point he told his internet–linked camera: 'I'll never do this again.'

Unfortunately for McAuley, weather turned far worse as he approached the South Island.

Two low pressure systems converged to produce 60 knot winds and 10–metre swells. He paddled to within 30kms of his target at Fiordland, where his wife and child were waiting. Then, late at night on February 9, search and rescue authorities received this radio message:

'Do you copy? This is *Kayak One*. Do you copy,

over? I've got an emergency situation. I'm in a kayak about 30 kilometres from Milford Sound.

'I need a rescue.

'My kayak's sinking . . . fell off into the sea and I'm going down.'

Helicopters could not be sent because winds were gusting to 80 knots. When the weather eased, the helicopters went in search and on February 10, they found the kayak part–filled with water.

'Casper' was missing and it was later assumed that the final part of his radio message indicated that 'Casper' had dragged McAuley and the boat down when hit by a freak wave. There was no sign of him and his body was never recovered.

≈   ≈   ≈

MEN BEGAN trying to row the Tasman Sea as far back as 1969 but no one was successful until Yorkshire–born New Zealander Colin Quincey made the 2,250km trip from New Zealand to Australia in his six–metre boat *Tasman Trespasser* in 63 days in 1977.

GPS did not exist at the time so navigation was by stars and compass.

His son Shaun was undoubtedly inspired by that

effort when he set out on an attempt to be the first person to make the reverse crossing in 2009. He took 54 days to row from New South Wales to Northland in *Tasman Trespasser II*. This was a 7.2–metre Kevlar-lined vessel with self–righting capability and solar panels to charge batteries that allowed webcasts.

His father had told Shaun of surfing down six–metre waves but that didn't deter the son. Hanging upside down after being rolled during a severe storm, and with the boat swamped so it wouldn't right, Shaun wondered what he was doing.

'There were some times there that were the lowest in my life — I didn't know how I was going to keep going,' he said afterwards.

He had good times too, seeing whales and dolphins.

'It just describes the Tasman — such a mixture of everything. One hour I'd be excited and happy about achieving a goal, and the next hour I'd be almost in tears and not knowing how I was going to keep going.'

He rowed from 7.30am to 11pm, taking breaks for food. The cabin was always wet. Bad weather reports sank his spirits.

'I knew it meant I was going to get thrown around for 24 hours a day, I was going to go backwards and there was nothing I could do about it. The whole trip was two steps forward and one and a half steps back.

Some days you'd row for 20 miles and you'd wake up and you'd gone backwards 21.'

He estimated he rowed about 4,000 kilometres.

He rowed into a sperm whale, capsized three times and broke two oars. His father's successful crossing inspired him at these times.

After rowing to the surf at 90 Mile Beach in 54 days, he abandoned ship and swam to shore and ordered a bacon and egg sandwich and a beer from the support crew that included his father.

'This is the best sandwich I've tasted in my life,' he said.

Married to Lisa and with one son, Shaun Quincey was asked if one day his boy might make the trip, to which he replied he 'wouldn't even let him think about it.'

≈   ≈   ≈

AUSTRALIANS Justin Jones and James Castrion who were mates from Sydney's Knox College were first to cross the Tasman in a kayak when they made the trip from Forster in New South Wales to Ngamotu Beach, New Plymouth, in 30 days, landing on January 13, 2008.

Their two-man boat was named *Lot 41*, after the

auction number under which the famous Kiwi–bred racehorse Phar Lap was sold to a buyer from across the Tasman. Their trip set a world record for the longest open–ocean voyage by kayak.

≈ ≈ ≈

TWO KIWIS were the first to kayak the 2,900km length of the Danube River from the Black Forest in Germany to the outlet into the Black Sea in Romania.

In 2010, multisport competitors Nick Riosa, 39, and Andrew Newick, 37, averaged 90 kilometres a day to cross eight countries in 31 days.

Riosa's Czech heritage inspired the adventure. The pair set out on June 8 and completed the trip on July 8, after paddling through a variety of obstacles including rapids, sewage, rubbish and the Serbian section where the riverbanks were still untouchable because of landmines laid during the war that broke up Yugoslavia.

'We were asked "Why?" a lot,' Riosa said. 'For me, it's always the challenge that appeals. It's doing something that has never been done before and pushing the limits. These crazy adventures, when you look back on them in your life, you can say you have achieved something extra,' he said afterwards.

Fishing trips

'There is nothing as relaxing as being out on the sea, listening to the waves and the wind in the sails, and the voices downstairs yelling, "How do you flush this toilet?" It takes a minimum of six people working in close harmony to successfully flush a nautical toilet. That's why those old sailing ships carried such a large crew.'

— Dave Barry, American satirist.

The shape of the coastline and the way that it merges with the water sometimes determines launch and landing methods.

I was taken by surprise and very nearly soiled my pants while making a return to shore after a fishing trip in Sydney with my mate Gary Foreman.

Given the rugged rocks, high cliffs and the surf that beats on Australia's east coast, there are very few boat ramps direct to the open ocean. The locals are used to exiting by estuary and river mouths and crossing bars, or going offshore from the safety of harbours.

The Long Reef boat ramp on Sydney's North Shore is one of a very few all the way from Victoria up to the Great Barrier Reef.

It can be a tricky launch when there is a swell pushing around the headland and into the south end of Collaroy Beach, with a steep wave that dumps on the boat ramp. But launching can be done quickly and, in a way, the bigger the surf, the better, because there is a greater interval between waves and between sets of waves.

It's a different story coming back in. There is not the time to back a trailer down, drive the boat onto it, secure it and get up the ramp in between sets of waves.

And so the locals pioneered a new system, which was put into practice and developed by several North Shore plumbers and builders with whom I worked.

Foreman and I had launched his five–metre runabout into a swell of less than half a metre but returned to the ramp after a successful day's fishing to find it was closer to a metre and a half. He stopped outside the surf line and had a good consideration of the conditions.

I was expecting him to seek better shelter further

inside the rock formation that gives Long Reef its name and then use his 4WD ute to retrieve the boat off the sand.

But suddenly he hit the throttle and when we came up to plane he pushed it full–on. We headed for the ramp at top speed.

The noise was such that I knew he wouldn't hear any question from me so I didn't bother, instead tucking myself down below the cockpit frame so that I didn't smash my face when the inevitable crunch came.

We gained air as we cleared the whitewater of broken waves and flew forward towards the next one, wobbling side–to–side at times, then hit the beach at a great rate of knots.

Foreman had the hydraulic lift on to raise the outboard as we sheared up the sand, beyond the reach of the waves and right next to the top end of the ramp, which slopes off both sides, inch–perfect.

He hopped out, ran the trailer back down the side of the ramp and winched the boat on.

I had the pleasure of teaching this method of retrieval to my son Jamey, a Sydney resident, at Long Reef in January 2010.

We were fortunate to have a calm day with just a small slop hitting the ramp. He had three runs at the sand before he got it right, spearing up far enough to be clear of the water and close enough to the ramp to allow easy winching onto the trailer.

One of those who first used the method was Shore swimming pool builder Peter Ryan, a dead–keen fisherman who regularly put to sea when surf was running and was something of a legend in terms of his catches.

On one occasion, he left into a small swell and returned to find a two–metre wave wrapping right onto the ramp. So he added extra speed going into the beach and his boat skidded right up the beach and onto grass next to the Long Reef Golf Club.

On the Wairarapa coast, the West Coast of the South Island and at Norfolk Island, fishing boats are launched from great heights via flying foxes and retrieved the same way so that they are clear of surf crashing into sheer cliffs.

≈   ≈   ≈

IT IS NOT UNCOMMON for fishermen to follow others who they think may know better.

The locals leading you to their secret spot, the regulars returning to areas where they've been making regular good catches, or tailing behind and taking a lead from the so–called experts. We left Pah Farm at

Fishing trips

Kawau Island on the Saturday of the annual Furuno Fishing Contest that had been held there for many years.

We were in a sponsored boat — yellow so it would stand out like dog's balls — and decked out with the logo of the *Fishing News* magazine.

And so it was that every time we pulled up at a spot we thought might be good, we were quickly spotted by some of the multitude of contest competitors (there were 3,000 of them in total) who thought we knew what we were doing.

As it turned out the electronics had been taken off the boat to avoid theft so we had no fish–finder or sounder. Photographer Glenn Jeffrey and I were out for a day seeking stories and photos, with a bit of fishing thrown in, as and when we could. But every time we pulled up anywhere, there would be a flow of 10 or more boats into whatever bay or offshore spot we were at.

We caught no fish that day, I suspect because of all the boat traffic.

≈   ≈   ≈

FISHERMEN often can't resist the urge to give each other a 'bum steer' as to where the fish are biting.

The query, 'Where did you catch them?' will often be met with bland replies such as, 'Just off the back of the boat.'

Don't believe all that you read in newspaper columns either.

Len Wong–Tam, who won the World Snapper Fishing Trophy at the Kawau Island contest one year, and whose son Tony also won it, used to provide fishing advice and commentary to the Saturday night sports paper *The 8–O'clock*.

'We'd send them all in the wrong direction and have a good chuckle about it,' he told me years later.

≈   ≈   ≈

BEFORE LEAVING the riverbank for a fishing excursion on the Corroboree Billabong in the Aboriginal territory of Kakadu, north of Darwin, the charter boat operator gave us the usual safety lecture.

He showed us where the lifejackets were stored, and then gave this advice: 'If the boat should go down, grab your lifejacket, work out where the nearest land is, throw the jacket as hard as you can in the opposite direction then swim as fast as you can to the shore. Hopefully, the crocodiles will go for the lifejacket — it's better to drown here than to be eaten by crocs.'

Fishing trips

TIM SHADBOLT had a meteoric rise to fame from concreter to Mayor of Waitemata City, where his beaming toothy smile and easy manner were avidly accepted.

At the time I had a mate, Roger Wakefield, who was reporting on West Auckland for the *NZ Herald* and he had struck up a friendship with the Mayor.

One day, Shadbolt loaned Roger his wooden home–made boat and I towed it out to Cornwallis on the Manukau Harbour for a fish.

We were out mid–channel just off Cornwallis, anchored in a fierce current but close to shore because we didn't much like the look of Shadbolt's boat in terms of its construction.

Sure enough, water began to seep through the hull in larger quantities than you can be comfortable with in a wooden boat.

Then the cleat to which the anchor was tied started to pop its screw out of the old, deteriorating and long–since paintless marine ply.

So we cut the line.

By this stage the boat had literally started to pull in two. We managed to nurse it back to shore, basically riding the current and using the two oars as rudders to send us in to land.

We beached at the far end of Cornwallis, where there

was no way to get the trailer in. The boat was broken and finished.

We rang Mayor Tim and he told us to retrieve what we could and what was useful and he'd send a couple of mates out to pick up the remainder for firewood.

I've still got the oars and rowlocks, the only parts of that boat that were sound when we had left shore.

Survivals

'As I have discovered by examining my past, I started out as a child. Coincidentally, so did my brother. My mother did not put all her eggs in one basket, so to speak; she gave me a younger brother named Russell, who taught me what was meant by "survival of the fittest".
— Bill Cosby, American comedian (1937–).

The Royal New Zealand Coastguard grew out of a proliferation of small local rescue groups, most of which were formed following some tragedy at sea.

The first official lifeboat organisation went into action in Timaru in 1864.

In 1976, the New Zealand Coast Guard Federation was established to bring all marine search and rescue groups under one umbrella organisation.

That made it possible for all groups to be heard as

one by government, sponsors and the public. The organisation has grown to 73 affiliated units including air patrols.

The coastguard is run by a board of nine, five of those appointed by the four national regions: North, Central, Canterbury and South, and four elected by members.

They run a multi–million dollar budget and an operation that includes many fulltime staff as well as more than 2,100 volunteers.

In the year to July 2010, the organisation received 3,666 calls for assistance. They involved 6,510 people. The coastguard was judged to have saved 31 lives and to have rescued 402 other people who had a variety of problems at sea.

Thirty lives were lost in incidents to which coastguard was called out. In addition, 327,408 radio calls were dealt with, including trip reports logged by its communications centres.

Coastguard volunteers spend 45% of their service time training, and 50% in patrolling, education and other public service.

It's estimated that only 5% of volunteers' time is actively involved in search and rescue operations.

The government provides around 15% of its funding through the National Rescue Coordination Centre, the rest coming from subscriptions from members, donations and community support.

At less than $100 a year to join, it's the best money a boatie can spend.

≈   ≈   ≈

PACIFIC ISLANDERS depend on the seas around them for sustenance and it is not uncommon for small boats to be blown offshore by unfavourable winds due to motor breakdown or other events.

The New Zealand and Australia Air Forces have been involved in many rescues of people who have been drifting helplessly at sea for days. It is incredible how many of these stories have a happy ending, thanks to the often calm seas.

Perhaps the most amazing of survival tales is that of three teenagers from the remote islands of Tuvalu. They were 50 days at sea in a small open boat without any water. The story took on new twists after their return to shore.

The trio left Atafu atoll on what was to be a short trip first said to be to fish, in their three–metre inflatable pontoon boat, taking just a few coconuts as food and drink. The wind changed, they were blown out to sea and had insufficient fuel to get back to land.

After three weeks during which relatives scoured the sea and the RNZAF conducted a wide aerial search to no avail, they were given up for dead by their community and their families held a memorial service for the boys, though no sign of them had been found.

On their 50th day at sea, 1,300kms from Tokelau and in the middle of the ocean far from shipping lanes, they were spotted by the Wellington–based Sanford boat *San Nikunau* which had been fishing in international waters.

First mate Tai Fredricsen said it was a 'pure miracle'. The *San Nikunau* was in waters it did not regularly fish. They saw the small craft dead–ahead.

'They were over the moon to see us.'

The fishing boat crew gave the boys fruit and water, bandaged their badly burned skin and shared their own clothes, which were all far too large for the emaciated trio. Next day they cooked them the traditional Kiwi breakfast of bacon, eggs, sausages and tomatoes.

They used their satellite 'phone to call the boys' relatives.

'I couldn't understand what they were saying, but I could tell they were ecstatic to find out the boys were still alive,' Fredricsen said.

'The boys had this incredible attitude, they survived so much.'

Survivals

The fishing boat made port at Suva, Fiji, two days later to off–load the teens. At the wharf one of the trio, Filo Filo,15, said he and his friends had almost given up hope just prior to being rescued.

'We were scared and praying was the only thing that kept us occupied every day. We slept, we went swimming and we talked, mostly about food. We had little hope that we would survive.'

He and his friends, Samu Pelesa, 15, and Etueni Nasau, 14, were taken to Suva Hospital for treatment for dehydration and sunburn sores.

'We survived because of God,' Filo Filo said on arrival at Suva. 'We managed to catch a few flying fish using our net and we also had a seagull which landed on the boat. We ate them raw.'

'The faces of our loved ones were what kept us going. We kept praying for a miracle,' he said.

Returned to family, they were taken on a tour of the Tokelaus to personally thank all those that had prayed for them.

And then came an addition to the story — they had originally left to get more vodka for a beach party. And shortly after, another fact — they had previously met some girls from another atoll and were hoping to catch up with them again.

Young love nearly killed them.

THE HAINAN, China–born Poon Lim holds the world record for longest solo feat of survival on a liferaft after being shipwrecked at sea for 133 days.

He was one of 55 sailors aboard the British freighter *SS Ben Lomond* bound from Cape Town to Guiana in South America in 1942 at the height of World War Two.

The ship was torpedoed by a German U–boat and sank.

Poon Lim managed to get aboard a life raft but did not see what happened to others. Some also made it to rafts and 11 were saved over progressive days — but not Poon Lim.

The raft contained several tins of biscuits, a bag of sugar cubes, 40 litres of fresh water, plus a torch and two smoke pots. He used the torch to attract fish and squid at night and snared them with hooks made from nails he prised from the raft. He caught rainwater in a tarpaulin.

After 133 days adrift he floated ashore at Belem in Brazil on April 5, 1943, half the Atlantic Ocean away from where the *Ben Lomond* went down.

When told no one had ever survived longer on a raft at sea, Poon Lim replied, 'I hope no one will ever have to break that record,' and almost seven decades later, no one had.

Survivals

SECOND-LONGEST survival in a liferaft was the 117 days spent by the British couple Maurice and Maralyn Bailey in a rubber lifering after their nine-metre yacht *Aralyn* was hit by a whale and sunk off the Galapagos Islands in Ecuador.

The Baileys had sailed from Europe through the Panama Canal and down the coast of South America in early 1973 and were intending to head for New Zealand when the accident happened.

They had no supplies and survived by collecting rainwater in a plastic sheet and by eating turtles and seabirds they could grab, plus fish they caught on safety pins taken from the raft's first aid kit.

Seven large ships passed within sight but without spotting them and meanwhile they drifted 2,400kms across the Pacific, until they were found by a Korean fishing trawler.

Unlike Poon Lim who had benefit of a solid hull underneath him and could stand on his own when he first arrived back on land, the Baileys had lost all muscle in their legs and had to be stretchered to hospital to recover.

≈　　　≈　　　≈

NEW ZEALAND'S most intriguing sea survival story involves the trimaran *Rose Noelle*. The boat belonged to John Glennie who had sailed the Pacific previously and, while berthed in Nelson, was seeking crew for a trip to Tonga in 1989.

He was joined by American James Nalepka, and Kiwis Rick Hellreigel and Phil Hoffman, none of whom was well acquainted with any of the others.

They had been at sea for a couple of days when they were hit by a storm off the Wairarapa coastline and the 12.6–metre, 6.5–tonne *Rose Noelle* was flipped.

The main compartment flooded after a hatch came off. The two outriggers were watertight and the men made for one of these where they sheltered.

For some unknown reason, the EPIRB distress signal they set off was not received. A search by the Royal New Zealand Air Force was targeted in the wrong area, too far north and near the Kermadec Islands, because they had not left a definite travel plan with anyone.

Glennie repeatedly dived into the main cabin to get the tins of food he had stored there and the fruit that was floating around. They collected rainwater.

After several weeks at sea, the hull grew barnacles and slime that attracted fish, and they used a gaff to haul kingfish aboard and drank the blood before eating them raw.

Survivals

On June 4, 1989, some 119 days after capsizing, the trimaran washed up at Little Waterfall Bay on Great Barrier Island in Auckland's outer Hauraki Gulf.

The crew clambered up a steep bush slope, broke into a remote bach, cooked themselves a meal and bedded down for a night.

Next day they telephoned the local police constable Shane Godinet to tell their remarkable story.

The four were airlifted by helicopter to the rescue base at Mechanics Bay in Auckland, where a huge media scrum including myself, then working for the *NZ Herald*, were waiting.

The survivors were skeletal. But that did not stop speculation they were lying, or that the trip had been a drugs run to South America gone wrong.

Eventually their story was accepted after examination of marine life attached to the hull and because of medical evidence of their condition.

The men had little in common when they left Nelson and did not keep in touch afterwards.

Hellreigel died of a brain tumour two years later. Glennie and Nalepka both moved to the United States while Hoffman moved from Picton to Mt Wellington in Auckland.

≈   ≈   ≈

THESE FEATS of survival involve not just courage, mental strength and ingenuity but strict self–control.

The three critical factors needed for survival are shelter, fresh water and food.

Drinking seawater will accelerate the process of death by dehydration, even if the saltwater is diluted with fresh water.

Likewise, drinking urine raises the body's salt content beyond what is healthy. Those who survive do so by drinking rainwater collected in covers and tarpaulins, or by drinking the blood of fish and turtles. The latter provide food.

Immersion in the water is quickly fatal, lowering the body temperature to the point where hypothermia sets in, then fatigue, then exhaustion followed by loss of the will to live.

Even in the tropics, life expectancy is just half a day, and survival time drops rapidly in colder water.

≈   ≈   ≈

SINCE THE LATE 1970s, surfers who discovered idyllic waves on remote islands of the Indonesian archipelago have turned the love of their life into a business by escorting other, paying tourists to these havens.

Survivals

Dangers have included the local sea snakes and reef sharks as well as the reefs themselves and the infections that invade coral cuts. There have been fires on board the converted Indonesian fishing trawlers, all wooden, as a result of cooking on dodgy gas stoves and barbeques.

But a group of Kiwis and Aussies on their 'trip of a lifetime' to the Mentawai Islands, off Sumatra, came home with a story to beat all others when they had to swim for their lives.

On October 24, 2010, a 7.5 magnitude earthquake struck south of the Mentawai Islands, producing a tsunami which sent three-metre-high waves washing through normally quiet harbours and estuaries.

Two surf excursion boats, the *Midas* and the *Freedom III* operated by a company called The Perfect Wave were anchored near each other in Macaroni's Bay for the night when the waves hit. The *Freedom III*, with six Sydney surfers aboard, was lifted violently and broke its mooring. Subsequent waves sent it hurtling into the *Midas*, which had eight surfers from the Gold Coast, two New Zealanders and five Indonesian crew members on board.

That caused the *Midas* to break its mooring and the collision also started a fire that within three minutes had turned the *Midas* into a blazing inferno.

While those on the *Freedom III* were able to turn their vessel around and head out to deeper water, the *Midas* was at the mercy of the tsunami waves.

Everyone jumped overboard. Some were picked up by the swells and thrown more than 200 metres inland, where they climbed trees while further waves came through.

The boat's Australian skipper, Rick Hallet, was one of them. Hallet said that when the earthquake struck, he heard an almighty roar.

'One of the surfers asked, "What is that?" I said, "Tsunami . . . " It hit us within a few seconds.'

They were among the lucky. At least 154 people died.

≈   ≈   ≈

TWO OF THE more common causes of death at sea are afflictions that at first seem quite manageable — toothache and seasickness.

There have been countless cases where a person has put to sea without any sign of tooth problems but without having had the regular maintenance that ensures oral health. Generally, the stages from toothache to death have been similar. A bad toothache turns into extreme pain and all the medicines aboard are quickly exhausted. Meanwhile, the poison from a bad abscess seeps into the blood system and the condition of the afflicted person quickly deteriorates until they are bedridden with fever.

From that point, and without powerful antibiotics, death can come within two days.

Charter skipper Rick Pollock tells of a deckhand who had to be airlifted off his boat *Pursuit* while on a trip to the Three Kings.

'We described the guy's condition to the hospital at Kaitaia by radio and they said he needed urgent attention. Later, when he was well, the hospital told us that another 24 hours and he would probably have been a goner.'

Likewise, those with serious sea–sickness can quickly succumb to dehydration followed by organ failure.

I've only ever been sea–sick once in my life but it was sufficiently bad for me to be able to sympathise with those who get the stomach rumbles every time they go near a boat. It happened on the way to the Chatham Islands aboard the Royal New Zealand Navy vessel *Manawanui*.

As we left Whitianga on the Coromandel Peninsula, a deep depression was moving up the country from the Southern Ocean. We had smooth sailing until we rounded East Cape, when the swells hit 10 metres, and the wind was 60 knots. It wasn't long before several crew, including the second in command, were hunched over the toilets throwing their stomachs out and there is nothing like the smell of vomit to bring on sea–sickness in others.

I joined them and spent much of the next 24 hours in the head. This was on the second floor of the five–storey boat, and the portholes showed nothing but green water which did nothing to help.

Eventually the skipper did the rounds of those who were crook to see if any needed medical attention. I asked him how to rid myself of the illness and his advice was to eat.

So off I went to the galley, where the cook warmed up some of the leftovers from dinner the night before — fatty lamb and boiled cabbage. I nearly chundered just looking at it but managed to get half the plate down before having to run for the head again.

I came back, finished the meal and made a quick recovery so the captain's advice was good. It's something I've believed ever since and passed on to those who fell ill on subsequent trips.

Sea–sickness is caused by imbalance in the inner ear, through which humans instinctively remain upright by maintaining a centre of gravity over their feet. The rolling motion of a boat upsets this balance as the lines that we use to register 'uprightness' — the mast, the windows, the run of the gunwales — are constantly in motion in reference to the land or the horizon. The motion also causes irregular pressures from the bowel against the diaphragm.

There are chemical means of controlling this, with medicines including Dimenhydrate, Scopalamine and Promethazine which are sold as ear patches or tablets under brand names including *Sea Legs*.

These cause drowsiness so ephedrine, used to make the illicit drug 'speed' or 'methamphetamine' is included in most and thus some are prescription medicines.

The best preventive I've come across is the 'Paihia Bomb,' made only at the pharmacy in Paihia by a husband–and–wife chemist team who hit on the formula while trying to help the many recreational boaties who travel around the Bay of Islands.

You can try natural ways to prevent or deal with the illness. Eat well before you leave port. Take sea–sickness medications well before you leave port. Don't drink alcohol.

If you feel sickness coming on, find a spot near the centre of gravity of the boat — the pendulum–like motion will be worst on higher points of the boat such as a flybridge.

Fresh air on the face helps. Keep your eyes fixed on the horizon. Think about anything other than sickness — for instance, steering the boat can help as it provides mental stimulus as well as an idea of the coming motion of the vessel.

Drink lots of water — if you do throw up, this will help prevent dehydration.

Chewing crystallised ginger helps some people. Others swear by cannabis and, in fact, pharmaceutical companies are attempting to produce an extract of the drug's Tetrahyrdracannabiloids (THC) as a sea-sickness remedy.

Wrist bands on the market claim to work by placing pressure on the P6 acupuncture point on the wrist but these have been scientifically tested and found to offer no benefit.

Researchers have tried various across-the-counter medications on their human 'guinea pigs' and, curiously, found there were similar results from the sea-sickness medications and from placebos including Vitamin C.

I have organised many offshore charter fishing trips to islands and mid-ocean reefs and I give the same advice to all participants who are nervous about getting sick, the ones who ask questions about it prior to departure.

I have no doubt that anxiety increases the likelihood of a bout of illness. 'If you think you'll get sick, you definitely will,' is my mantra.

≈ ≈ ≈

THE TALE OF the takeover of the *Bounty* and the banishment of her master Captain Bligh and his officers to a rowboat is etched in history as perhaps the most famous mutiny of all time.

Bligh is an interesting character, described by some historians as 'misunderstood and complex.' He clearly is not the monster portrayed in the movies.

Interestingly, the facts in this case are better than the fictionalisation and they should have stuck to them.

Bligh was born in 1754 in Cornwall to a seafaring family and at age seven was apprenticed to the Royal Navy, finally going to sea at age 16.

By age 22 he was sailing with Captain James Cook on the South Pacific voyage of discovery aboard *Resolution* and he was the ship's master with Cook's third expedition, when Cook was killed in Hawaii.

In 1788, Bligh set out for Tahiti on the *Bounty*, his mission to take on a cargo of breadfruit trees and transport them to the West Indies, where they were to be planted to provide food for slaves transported from

Africa. He tried three times to get around Cape Horn and was driven back by storms and so sailed around the Cape of Good Hope to get to Tahiti.

By then, it was too late to take the cargo and so they had to wait eight months for the next season's breadfruit to grow.

The crew apparently became accustomed to the local customs which included free sexual association and a relaxed lifestyle in the sunshine.

And so a few days after they sailed from Tahiti and headed for the Caribbean in April 1789, the second watch, led by the master's mate, Fletcher Christian, raided the armoury and took all the weapons.

They then cornered Bligh and trussed him up.

Those loyal to him surrendered and so there was no bloodshed. They were offered the chance to go with their captain in a seven–metre lifeboat and 14 did so. They were given food and water to last a few days, a sextant and a watch, but no compass.

Bligh sailed back towards Tahiti and landed at Tofua atoll where they collected water and food. One crewman was killed in a fight with the locals and as they had no weapons, they set to sea again, bypassing Fiji because they feared a similar encounter.

Bligh steered for the only nearby European community, the Portuguese in Timor, and made the

6,700km journey in 47 days, a remarkable feat. He returned to England.

HMS Pandora, commanded by Edward Edwards, was dispatched to run down the mutineers. Fletcher Christian, meanwhile, had sailed back to Tahiti, married a local girl, dropped off 14 of the *Bounty* crew and then set sail to evade capture. He and his wife, five other mutineers, six Tahitian men and five other Tahitian women settled down on remote Pitcairn Island.

Edwards captured 14 mutineers at Tahiti and locked them in a cage on *Pandora*'s deck, in searing heat. The ship hit Great Barrier Reef while sailing to the penal colony in New South Wales, and sank.

The prisoners would all have drowned if the bosun's mate had not unlocked their cage before jumping overboard. All the same, 31 crew and four prisoners died.

Edwards rounded up the rest and they were sent back to England where four were acquitted thanks to evidence from Bligh that they were not complicit in the mutiny. Three were found guilty of not resisting the mutiny and were pardoned. Three were hanged.

Meanwhile, on Pitcairn, the relationship between the six Englishmen, the six Tahitian men and the six Tahitian women was exploding in violence.

When the next Europeans arrived there in 1808, only one mutineer and the six women were alive. Ten of the men had died in fights over the women and another had fallen from a cliff while drunk.

Bligh was court–martialled for the loss of the *Bounty* but acquitted. He faced two further court martials in his naval career and all charges were dismissed, allowing him to rise to the rank of Vice Admiral. After the Battle of Copenhagen in 1801, he was praised for his seamanship and leadership by the Admiral Lord Nelson.

One historian summed up Bligh's weaknesses: 'He saw fools about him too easily. Thin–skinned vanity was his curse through life. He never learnt that you do not make friends of men by insulting them.'

≈ ≈ ≈

THE GREATEST sea survival saga of all time is surely that of Ernest Shackleton and his men during their Antarctic exploration after their ship *Endurance* was crushed by sea ice.

I've had the privilege of touring the huts of the early Antarctic explorers after working 'on the ice' in 1996. The feeling of history is palpable, embedded in the cracked weatherboards.

Survivals

After sailing south, Shackleton and his men spent nine months stuck in ice in the Ross Sea and a further six months camped on a drifting ice floe. When that floe broke up, the group was forced to take to lifeboats for a five–day row to land on remote Elephant Island, far from the routes of the whalers and sealers who were their only hope of rescue.

And so Shackleton and three others set off in the best of the lifeboats with little food and only basic navigational aids to try to reach the Norwegian whaling station at South Georgia Island, about 600kms away, and did so.

Shackleton was of lowly Irish descent and his feats during the period of 'Great Antarctic Exploration' were overshadowed by those of the wealthy and well–connected Englishman, Captain Robert Falcon Scott.

It was not until the late 20th century that his story became widely known and he cornered the reputation as the better and greater explorer.

He cut his teeth in the cold climate as third officer with Scott's first expedition from 1901–1904 but was sent home early due to severe influenza.

He vowed to return. Scott extracted a promise from Shackleton that the latter would not use the base at McMurdo Sound that Scott had set up on their first trip together.

Shackleton complied, and in 1909 led an expedition that established a far better accommodation from which he launched a march to within 190kms of the South Pole, further south than anyone else had been.

His party was the first to traverse the South Polar Plateau and the first to climb Mt Erebus.

They extended their exploration to the ultimate and had to race time and starvation to make it back to McMurdo Sound in time to get the ship out before winter set in.

They were on half–rations for much of the way and nearing the end, Shackleton gave his one biscuit allotted for the day to Frank Wild, who was sick.

Wild later wrote in his diary: 'All the money that was ever minted would not have bought that biscuit and the remembrance of that sacrifice will never leave me.'

That act of loyalty to his men was repeated in many different ways by the party leader on future expeditions.

Shackleton was knighted by King Edward VII. In 1912, the Norwegian Roald Amundsen beat Scott to the Pole and the latter, who had earlier been knighted for his exploits, perished in the attempt.

The last great achievement available to explorers was to cross Antarctica side–to–side via the Pole and

Shackleton set out to do that. He was about to leave port when World War One broke out on August 3, 1914, but the Lord of the Admiralty, Winston Churchill, ordered that the partly government-sponsored expedition go ahead.

Shackleton's ship, *Endurance*, left Portsmouth on August 8. Last landfall before the Frozen Continent was South Georgia. They sailed from there in early January, intending to make land and off-load supplies that would get them beyond the Pole. Meanwhile, another ship, the *Aurora*, was to drop men and supplies on the opposite side of the 2,900km-wide continent so an advance party could leave food stores at regular intervals and be prepared for the arrival of the transcontinental party.

That summer was particularly cold. Shackleton couldn't get close enough to solid land to unload and set up camp.

On January 19, 1915, *Endurance* became stuck fast in sea ice. It drifted in the ice, being squeezed and cracked until October 24, when water rushed in and the crew shifted onto the ice.

They removed everything they could in the following days, tore the ship apart and set up a decent camp shelter on the ice floe. *Endurance* sank on November 21.

The crew drifted on the floe until April 9, when the ice island split in two and showed signs of cracking up.

Shackleton ordered the lifeboats from the ship to be deployed and after a five–day row and a total of 497 days at sea since they had left South Georgia, the exhausted men arrived at Elephant Island.

They knew they would not survive there. Aside from the cold, the only food was seals and sea birds and the only water came from boiled snow. Their supplies, including matches, were running low.

While on the island Shackleton gave his mittens to photographer Frank Hurley who was there to record the exploration for posterity, because Hurley had lost his own mittens. On the subsequent journey seeking rescue, he suffered frostbite as a result.

Shackleton decided to take the best of the lifeboats, named the *James Caird* after one of his sponsors, and tried to sail to South Georgia with three others, leaving 22 men on Elephant Island.

The carpenter from the *Endurance*, Harry McNish, raised the sides of the lifeboat and made a shelter from parts of the other boats and their sails. McNish was chosen to accompany Shackleton in the aim for South Georgia because of his skills and despite having earlier argued vehemently with Shackleton about a variety of problems when they were stuck on the ice floe. Shackleton chose the captain of the *Endurance*, Frank Worsley, for his navigational skills and the three of the crew he judged to be the strongest: Tom Crean, John Vincent and Jim McCarthy.

They took with them enough food and water for four weeks because Shackleton expected that if they had not found land within that time, they would be dead.

They left Elephant Island on April 24, 1915, and landed at South Georgia on May 8, thanks to extraordinary seamanship from Worsley who had only brief navigational fixes by sextant because of constant cloud cover at night. But they arrived within sight of land during a ferocious Southern Ocean storm and had to stay at sea because of the danger of being dashed on rocks.

When they finally made landfall after 24 hours it was on the opposite side of the island from the whaling base and seas were so rough, there was no chance they could get offshore again.

Shackleton chose Worsley and Crean as the strongest members of the party with whom to cross the mountainous island and they climbed up and down for 36 hours before arriving at Stromness.

Shackleton knocked on the door of the Norwegian

commander of the station who he knew from previous visits.

'Who are you?' the man asked.

'Ernest Shackleton,' was the reply. The commander at first did not believe him because the expedition had been given up as lost more than a year before.

Shackleton then made two attempts to get to the other side of South Georgia by boat during the storm before he was successful on the third, as seas calmed.

He retrieved McNish, Vincent and McCarthy. Then he convinced the Chilean Navy to help in the rescue of the men at Elephant Island and that country's government obliged by sending the navy tug *Yelcho*, which arrived on August 30, 1915, and picked up all 22 men safely.

They were black from the soot of the seal blubber they had burned for warmth in their shelter under the hulls of the upturned lifeboats. They had cooked blubber for meals and used seal skins to stay warm.

Shackleton's next mission was to go back to the Ross Sea to get the men who had been dropped off by *Aurora* after laying a food trail and were supposed to have been picked up by *Endurance*. Three had died during the repeated food–laying trips.

Shackleton returned to England with all but those three, the rest all having endured extreme deprivation.

Survivals

He dreamed of further exploration but heavy drinking and bad health overtook his desire.

He was leading another Antarctic trip and was at South Georgia again on January 5, 1922, when he suffered a fatal heart attack.

His body was in the process of being returned to England when news came that his wife Emily believed he should be buried at South Georgia. His doctor, Alexander Macklin — who had conducted the autopsy after death and determined that it was due in part to the exertions Shackleton had undergone and in part to heavy drinking — took his body there.

On 5 March, 1922, Shackleton was buried in the Grytviken cemetery, South Georgia, after a short service in the Lutheran church.

'I think this is as "the Boss" would have had it himself,' Macklin later wrote in his diary, 'standing lonely in an island far from civilisation, surrounded by stormy tempestuous seas, and in the vicinity of one of his greatest exploits.'

I've been to both Scott's first shelter still known as Hut Point, to his much better appointed hut at Cape Evans and to Shackleton's hut at Cape Royds.

Hut Point is built on black rock at the edge of the sea, which it thaws in the brief summer. Because of the easy landing, the Americans subsequently established their McMurdo base there and today it accommodates up to 3,000 people over the summer. These include researchers looking at the ozone hole and climate change, trying to find enzymes to assist those with heart problems from fish whose blood does not clot in the cold, and a myriad of other projects, supported by a huge crew of transport and other staff including cooks, who are highly valued by the Antarctic workers.

In the summer months I was there, the temperature occasionally hit 20 degrees on cloudless, windless days and you could walk around quite comfortably in jeans and a T-shirt.

But you didn't want to be near Hut Point on those days as it stank worse than a landfill does in 40 degree heat.

In 2010, carpenters with the New Zealand Antarctic Heritage Trust were restoring floorboards at Shackleton's hut at Cape Royds when they found unopened cases of McKinlay's scotch whisky which had been stored there since 1909.

'The whisky is a gift from heaven for whisky lovers,' said Richard Paterson of the modern-day McKinlay's company, which still produces scotch.

Some was returned to the company so it could analyse the liquor as it was said to have done nothing but improve in taste.

Work boats

'When men come to love a sea life, they are not fit to live on land.'
— *Samuel Johnson (1709–1784).*

The biggest ship ever built was the 458–metre –long *Seawise Giant*, an oil tanker that weighed 81,879 tonnes unladen and had a total displacement of 657,019 tonnes.

She was too big to go through the Suez or Panama Canals and her 24–metre draft prevented navigation in the English Channel.

The Korean–built ship had a short life. After launch in 1989 it quickly became obvious that she was just too big for ocean travel. And so she was sold to an oil terminal in Qatar, which moored her for nine years until 1999, when land–based facilities replaced her capacity.

She was then towed to Alanga in the Gujarat Province in India and driven onto the beach then cut up for scrap.

≈   ≈   ≈

THE LARGEST pure 'work boat' in the world is the Dutch–owned *Giant 4*, a semi–submersible ocean–going lifting and transport platform.

It is 140 metres long and 36 metres wide, with just a small forward bridge that allows sufficient deck space behind it to seat a full oil drilling platform.

Giant 4 was called to Murmansk, Russia, when the nuclear submarine *Kursk* sank on the seabed, to recover the hull.

≈   ≈   ≈

THE WIDEST and tallest ships on the Seven Seas and those with the most load–carrying capacity are the United States' aircraft carriers, beaten in length only by the Copenhagen, Denmark–based Maersk shipping company's E–class containers ships, by just a few metres.

These and their array of support and protection craft are sent to troublespots around the world at the first signs of tension. They allow the US to back up their own and their allies' land–based forces without requiring either airports on land or permission to use them, and the adage in modern warfare is that he who controls the air, wins the war.

And because carrier groups are the first military dispatched in times of international tension, spotters are these days invited to report carrier group movements on internet sites including 'Where are the Carriers?'

Since the *USS Enterprise* was built in 1961, she and all carriers built subsequently have been labelled super–carriers and all boast roughly the same statistics. They are roughly 343 metres in length and 75 metres wide wing–to–wing, providing 1,672 square metres of deck space.

The wings are the 'parking areas' where planes wait prior to take–off or are taken on landing and ahead of stowage below decks, via elevator.

Existing carriers include the *USS Enterprise* and 11 others, nine named for US Presidents – the *George Washington*, *Abraham Lincoln*, *Theodore Roosevelt*, *Dwight D. Eisenhower*, *Harry S. Truman*, *John F. Kennedy*, *Gerald Ford*, *Ronald Reagan* and the *USS George H.W. Bush* — and two after naval officers — the *Carl Vinsen* and the *Nimitz*.

They typically carry around 13,000 crew, from engineers and cooks to armourers and pilots, as well as a resident marine battalion.

Steam–powered catapults launch fully fuelled and armed planes weighing up to 48 tonnes from zero to 160mph in two seconds.

Four steel 'arrestor' drag cables laid across the deck catch hooks dangling off the tail of landing aircraft and the catapult absorbs the tension to bring them from 150mph to stop in three seconds and within 100 metres of deck. In daylight, the crews can launch two aircraft and retrieve one every 37 seconds. At night they can launch one and retrieve one every 60 seconds.

On landing, the deck lights transmit a radar–like beam to incoming planes and provide a Heads Up Display (HUD) on the windscreen, with a horizontal green line at which approach height is ideal, with orange warning lights for two high and red for two low. A flashing red signal is a 'wave away,' the order to go around again.

The typical super–carrier air wing features three squadrons (10 aircraft) of FA–18 Hornet fighter/bombers, one squadron of F14 Tomcat fighters (the plane Tom Cruise flies in *Top Gun*), one Viking submarine finder–and–destroyer, and one squadron of Sea Hawk helicopters for ferrying the marines. In the air at all times is the ship's E–2C Hawkeye radar plane with an eight–metre diameter rotating dome that provides early warning of attackers and allows advice on trouble–free attack routes.

The Viking is also able to carry and deliver fuel to the Hawkeye and to attacking planes while airborne.

Also guarding the carrier will be two guided missile cruisers, one guided missile destroyer, one anti–submarine destroyer and an anti–submarine frigate and two submarines. And tailing these will be a re–supply ship carrying fuel and ammunition.

The nuclear–powered carriers can leave the rest of the fleet behind in any sort of weather, capable of steaming at 30–plus knots. They burn money fast: each costs in the vicinity of US$1 billion per month in running costs, maintenance and wages.

The *Enterprise* was expected to be retired in 2013 and another super–carrier was already under construction to replace her.

≈   ≈   ≈

FISHERMEN ARE a tough bunch, no–nonsense types. They work hard, play hard. Stories of their antics in port abound.

One Far North bloke would 'fill his boots' at sea for days and then, cashed up, head for the nearest bar to do the same. His trick was to get a couple down quickly, then bet the locals he could drink down all the cigarette butts and other discarded goodies in the bar's ashtrays in a gumboot of beer.

He'd empty the trays in the boot, get the barman to fill it off the tap, then stand at the bar and down the lot. It was $10 each against his fat pay. He never lost.

At Mangonui in the Far North, there was a certain local woman who had a penchant for sailors and 'easy' didn't even begin to describe her antics.

She was riddled with sexual diseases, the signs of which were etched on her face — as one fisherman described her, she had 'skankers the size of saucers'.

Of course, she'd still get lucky now and then with a drunkard who had been at sea for a while. One night in the bar she picked her target, a young deckhand, and made it clear to him what she wanted.

Subject to much ribbing from his crewmates, he made it clear he wasn't interested.

She persisted, to no avail. But when the deckie got back to the boat moored at Mangonui Wharf and went to his bunk, there she was, already under the blankets and waiting for him.

She refused to get out. So he unwound the fire hose,

took it into his cabin and turned it on high pressure, literally blowing her out of his sleeping quarters.

A group of transvestites and transsexuals used to hang around in the old Great Northern Hotel, now long gone, at the downtown end of Auckland's Queen St, where foreign sailors would get their first drinks when on shore leave. They'd try to sell themselves, and some would try to entice a half–cut sailor, and every now and then a fight would break out.

Sometimes the 'girls' would gang up on a target and attack and rob him.

After one such incident, three of these drag queens were arrested and charged with assault and robbery and they ended up in the Auckland District Court.

I was working for the *Truth* newspaper at the time and the editor sent myself and a photographer to court to get the story. The picture snapper, Dan Machiavelli, was concealed behind a large oak tree in the park across the road from the front door of the court waiting for the trio to emerge after their appearance. As they did, he popped out and shot off several frames.

They saw him, flipped off their high–heels and gave chase, running him down easily because he had his heavy camera bag. They took to Dan's head with their heels, leaving his skull looking like a timber floor that's been at the mercy of a woodpecker, and one ripped the sleeve from his suit jacket clean off at the shoulder before police intervened.

≈   ≈   ≈

YOU WOULDN'T want to be an Asian crewman on a vessel working the oil run from the Arab states and around the east African coast to markets in South East Asia these days.

In 2010, there were 164 hijacking attacks on major cargo vessels, 37 vessels were seized, more than 700 sailors taken hostage and 12 killed, 16 injured.

Somali pirates operating in small, fast inflatable boats and converted fishing trawlers launched armed attacks on nearly 1,000 ships passing the Horn of Africa between Yemen and Kenya in the decade from 2000.

The largest vessel hijacked was a South Korean mega–tanker, the *Samho Dream*, which was held from April until November 2010 before its owners agreed to a payment of US$9.5 million, the money flown to inland Somalia before the 24 crew were allowed to regain control of the vessel and her US$160 million cargo of crude oil. A South Korean gunboat stood offshore in deeper water to escort the ship to safe harbour.

Work boats

Great Britain, France, the United States and other European and Asian countries have had warships patrolling the seas off Somalia since 2005 and they have deterred many attacks and intervened in others, often engaging in fire–fights with the raiders.

Some shipping companies have paid mercenaries to guard their vessels and on numerous occasions these guards have fought off pirate attacks where the small boats are driven next to the hull of the ships and grappling hooks and rope ladders used to board them.

Passenger ships have also been targeted, in one case the skipper manoeuvring in a series of zig–zags which eventually resulted in the huge ship's wake overturning the pirates' boat.

After the *Samho Dream* incident, the British Government began a new programme of employing former SAS soldiers at a rate of £1,500 per week to ride aboard as escort through the danger region.

The ex–Special Forces troops also began training Somali Government troops. This had been tried and abandoned earlier in the decade, large numbers of the trainees deciding there was more money to be made on the other side and taking their new expertise, weapons and equipment with them when they deserted to join pirate groups.

Somali pirates are also subject to the first piracy charges laid by the United States since 1903. Five Somalis got more than they bargained for when they mistook the US Navy's 138−metre destroyer *USS Nicholas* for a merchant ship. They pulled alongside in a small boat and fired shots from rifles.

The *Nicholas* responded with a burst of heavy cannon fire that sent the boat skittering for shore and later sank it, and all those on board were arrested.

≈   ≈   ≈

MANY PEOPLE gamble on the ocean. In the United States, many more gamble on the Mississippi River.

It's nothing new. As the Southern Baptist and other religions took strong hold in the Southern States, alcohol, and the 'carousing' in saloons that provided brothels and gambling, came under attack.

And so those running those rackets took to the water where state laws didn't apply, and where there were plenty of travelling customers, merchants and salesmen, with time on their hands. Riverboat gambling is legend down the Mississippi.

The author Samuel L. Clemens took his pen−name from the lingo used by the deck hands on the paddle steamers, where he had some experience early in life

— where the river and its berths were low, a forward lookout would feel the depth under the boats by use of a pole with depth measured in fathoms: 'Mark' was the call when the measuring was being done, and 'Twain' meant two fathoms underneath and signalled sufficient depth to keep going.

And gambling scenes feature in many of Mark Twain's stories and books.

Today, the gambling laws are varied and very confused.

On land, only a few states including Nevada where the nation's gaming capital, Las Vegas, is located allow casino gambling.

Some casinos are built on Indian reservations inside some of the states that ban gambling but these are governed by Federal rather than state laws. No anti-gambling legislation applies to waterways.

Since 1990, the floating casinos have become increasingly popular with state governments keen to take easy pickings in taxes, while maintaining a holier-than-thou stance for their solid Baptist electorates. By 2011, 72 such gambling boats were at work, all built in the old paddle steamer style to add a touch of class.

They provide one-armed bandits, the card games blackjack and poker and roulette, but none of the other games common on land.

The boats conduct gambling 'sessions', berthing to let customers on and off then steaming mid–stream, but never too far from the wharf.

The law stipulates that they must not be tied up while gambling takes place — unless the captain considers that weather or other conditions would endanger the passengers, in which case they can allow gambling while tied up; a slight breeze can now be judged sufficiently dangerous to stay berthed and save the fuel.

≈   ≈   ≈

IN THE OLD DAYS, the seabeds and coastlines of the world were mapped by sextant and plumbob.

The latest technology involves an unmanned, remotely controlled submersible craft about the size of a large surfboard.

Oceanographers in Australia developed the *Seaglider*, a solar–powered and battery–driven 'boat' that can spend months at sea collecting information on water temperature, current flow, salinity, dissolved oxygen and turbidity while also drawing the shape of the seabed and recording water depth.

It was sent into the Coral Sea to the north of the country prior to Christmas 2010 and spent 149 days profiling the waters between Darwin and East Timor. The *Seaglider* covered 3,000kms and made 768 dives.

The craft is controlled from a base in Perth as part of an Australian Federal Government programme called the Integrated Marine Observation System. The aim is to both improve sea chart mapping and to collect data related to marine climate.

The only problem during *Seaglider*'s first foray was an attack by a large tiger shark, which retreated after crunching its teeth on the stainless steel casing.

≈   ≈   ≈

THE WRECKAGE of the *Titanic* was found by Frenchman Jean–Louis Michel and the American Dr Robert Ballard. The latter has a long and colourful history and is now the world's best–known oceanographer.

It is rumoured his success in finding shipwreck sites that evaded others is down to connections within the United States Navy, who supply him with information discovered during tracking of the ocean bed by the navy's nuclear submarines as they move continuously around the globe.

Ballard was born in Kansas in 1942. His father worked on the *US Minuteman* nuclear missile programme for American Aviation and Robert worked for the company for many years.

He first joined the army where he was seconded to the intelligence section, then transferred to the navy because of his fascination with the sea.

'Captain Nemo in *20,000 Leagues Under the Sea* by Jules Verne is who I always wanted to be,' he once said.

'Absolutely no doubt about it. I always had this dream of being inside his ship, the *Nautilus*.'

The intel connection saw him posted as liaison between Naval Research and the Woods Hole Oceanographic Institute. He left the naval service in 1970 but held the rank of Commander and was later called up for specific operations, including a job that led to discovery of *Titanic*.

The navy desperately wanted to find two nuclear-powered and nuke torpedo–carrying submarines that had been lost at sea. The *USS Thresher* went down off the coast of New England in 1963 and the *USS Scorpion* sank mid–Atlantic in 1967 and the reasons for their loss was not clear, theories including Soviet sabotage or attack.

In 1977, Ballard had made his first, unsuccessful search for *Titanic*. By the early 1980s, he was developing means of deep–sea exploration and his remotely controlled robot Argo clinched a navy–funded deal whereby the vessel *Knorr,* owned by the Woods Hole Institute, would first search for the submarines and photograph them and then look for the passenger liner.

In 1985, Ballard found all three vessels.

He discovered the wreck of the German battleship *Bismarck* in water 5kms deep in 1989. Nine years later, he found the *USS Yorktown,* sunk by Japanese bombs during the Battle of Midway in June 1942.

In 2002, he found the PT torpedo boat *109* commanded by John F. Kennedy who would later become US President, which was rammed by a Japanese battleship off the Solomon Islands.

More recently he was involved in sonar scanning and submersible exploration of the Black Sea, finding sailing vessels that traded in the area back to 4500BC.

≈ ≈ ≈

ALL VESSELS have a limited lifetime. An average lifetime for freight carriers is 30 years, by which time it becomes uneconomical to refit and/or repair them, and this is compounded by advances in technology which give fuel savings.

About 95% of the world's retired marine fleet ends

up in India, Bangladesh or Pakistan for breaking up and recycling.

Half of that goes to Alang in the Gujarat province on the north–west coast of India.

Hundreds of old cargo and container vessels, fishing boats and ferries are moored offshore awaiting dismantling.

The ships are brought ashore on spring high tides and then thousands of workers set on them with cutting equipment to salvage steel and any useable parts.

Similar scenes take place at Chittagong in Bangladesh and at Gadani in Pakistan.

The reason the work is done primarily in these three places is the low labour cost and the lack of labour and environmental laws in relation to the toxic chemicals the boats contain.

These vary from fuel and greasing oils to contaminated bilge water, asbestos insulation, and PCBs and dioxins in generators.

Other harmful effects include the lead paints, and anti–fouling from the hulls which leaches into the beach.

Prior to the shipwrecking business, which was only back in 1983, Alang was said to be pristine. Now, the beach is oil–stained over a strange orange colour, as is the water, and there is no sign of marine life.

Work boats

In 2006, Greenpeace focused attention on the environmental damage when it took court action to prevent the old French aircraft carrier *Clemenceau* being broken up when it was taken there.

Indian and French courts upheld the Greenpeace case and the *Clemenceau* was ordered back to France, where it stood on a mooring for two years until a British company based at Hartlepool agreed to scrap her, with agreement from the environmental lobby group which approved of the wrecking and recycling plan.

≈ ≈ ≈

Boaties' Tales

Floating gold

'The barge she sat in, like a burnished throne, Burned on the water: the poop was beaten gold; Purple the sails, and so perfumed that The winds were lovesick with them; the oars were silver, Which to the tune of flutes kept stroke, and made The water which they beat to follow faster, As amorous of their strokes.'
— *writer William Shakespeare, from* Antony and Cleopatra.

Australasia's wealthiest man owns Australasia's flashiest recreational boat. Food and packaging multi–billlionaire Graeme Hart's 'yacht', the *Ulysses*, does not have a sail but it does feature accommodation for 14 guests in seven staterooms each with their own head, separate quarters for eight crew, a restaurant–sized kitchen, a spa pool, storage for jetskis, kayaks and rubber inflatables and a helipad.

The keel of the 58–metre boat was laid in 2000 at Trinity Yachts in New Orleans. It went to San Diego for electronics fitting prior to shipment to New Zealand via a purpose–built boat carrier.

But when it was near completion in 2002, fire swept through the *Ulysses*.

It went back to New Orleans for a rebuild and refit that took six years. By 2011, its worth was estimated at $100 million.

But this was just one of Hart and wife Robyn's toys. They also owned a 32–metre yacht also named *Ulysses*.

And while en route to his Waiheke Island mansion one day, Hart saw the brand new police cutter swishing across the Waitemata Harbour. He envisaged one for himself and ordered a replica hull and superstructure with luxury interior.

The result was the U–21, a 20–metre fibreglass vessel with large saloon and galley and a spiral staircase to the wheelhouse, driven by four V8–powered water jets that make it capable of 50 knots — probably New Zealand's fastest fishing boat.

It was designed and built by the firms that produced the police launch, Technicraft and Composite Projects. The cops' boat cost just under $3 million while Hart's boat cost more than $8 million.

Floating gold

HART'S BOATS pale in comparison to those owned by 'Admiral' Roman Abramovich — or Abramovich's Navy as it is known in Europe.

Just in time for Christmas in 2010, he took delivery of *Eclipse*, the world's largest privately owned 'yacht'. According to industry experts, the 560 foot (170–metre) vessel was specifically designed and named to overshadow what was previously the world's largest private yacht, a 525–footer owned by Sheikh Mohammed bin Rashid Al Maktoum, the ruler of Dubai.

Oil magnate and Chelsea Football Club owner Abramovich spent $1.2 billion on *Eclipse* which was built by Blohm and Voss in Hamburg, Germany.

It features luxury accommodation for 30, two swimming pools, several on–board tenders and two helipads, so Abramovich's personal chopper doesn't have to move when guests fly in or out.

More unusually, it has a submarine that can be released via an escape hatch in the hull so he can arrive and leave unannounced. A circular 'sunken conversation pit', where hull plates slide back, allows underwater viewing from lounge chairs.

Defences include a state–of–the–art military anti–missile system and bullet proof windows, plus an 'anti–paparazzi' photo shield system, while Abromovich's personal suite takes up the full 22–metre beam of the boat and is encased in armour plating. *Eclipse* is said to feature $350 million worth of luxury fittings. Among these are a wallpaper made from the skin of manta rays.

At 2011 prices, it cost about $220,000 to fill up the diesel tanks and the annual maintenance bill was in the vicinity of $45 million.

Until 2010, the pride of Abramovich's Navy was the 115–metre *Pelorus*. He owned the 112–metre *Le Bleu* until 2009 when he gave it to friend and business associate Eugene Shvidler. The 98–metre *Ecstasea* was fitted out in Chinese style and he would use that for short trips out from England. In addition, the fleet also contained the 115–metre sailing yacht *Luna* moored ready for use in Norway and the 50–metre *Sussaro* which he kept in The Antibes.

≈　　≈　　≈

SOME OF THE world's biggest super–yachts have facilities that rival major hotels.

The *Al Said*, owned by Sultan Kaboos of Oman, has a concert hall that seats a 50–piece orchestra as well as 200 guests. Seventy guests can stay on board, and 150 crew are there to serve them.

Floating gold

The *Constellation*, owned by the ruling family of Qatar, has a fleet of four wheel drive vehicles, a submarine, a helicopter pad, and features sea fossils embedded in walls and tables.

The *Dubai*, owned by Mohammed bin Rashid Al Maktoum, Prime Minister of the United Arab Emirates, has two squash courts and a fleet of recreational fishing vessels.

The five storey *Ambrosia*, built for an American media magnate but recovered by receivers for re–sale, has a spa pool outside behind the top–deck wheelhouse which overflows to the swimming pool on the deck below.

If you desire a cruise on a multi–billionaire's 'yacht', you could rent the *Rosehearty,* put out to lease in the Mediterranean and the Caribbean by its owner, News Corporation chairman Rupert Murdoch.

The 56–metre three–master includes five suites each with their own ensuite, a gymnasium, fishing and dive gear, and two six–metre tenders named *Grace* and *Chloe* after Murdoch's latest offspring.

As part of any deal, prospective hirers would have use of a crew of eight in starched white linens emblazoned with the vessel's name to provide the meals, do the washing–up and the laundry, as well as sail the boat and mix cocktails.

Among those who have enjoyed a stay — and forked out the $350,000 weekly fee — are actor Mel Gibson, singer Billy Joel and the British PM, David Cameron.

Billionaire businessman Larry Ellison has owned two boats with basketball courts — the *Katana* and *Rising Sun* — though he put the latter up for sale in 2010, saying it was 'too big and lacked intimacy'.

Of Ellison, the world's ninth richest man at the time, American satirist Dave Barry said: 'He's a boating enthusiast, although that seems too weak to describe his level of interest, kind of like describing someone as "a heroin fancier"'.

≈ ≈ ≈

IGOR IS A RUSSIAN immigrant to New Zealand, a businessman who shifted plenty of money over. He bought a big house in the Bay of Islands. He went fishing with some locals and loved it. So he bought a big boat. But he knew nothing about boating and after fishing in a spot the locals had introduced him to, he couldn't retrieve his anchor. It was jammed solid.

He telephoned one of the boys who had taken him out and asked for advice.

He was told to slacken the rope off, move the boat around to different angles and try to free it from a different direction. He did, but couldn't. And so he cut the anchor rope and left the $3,000 stainless steel anchor wedged on a reef.

He went back the next day with a new one. He dropped it and it, too, stuck fast in the rock. He telephoned for advice again and was told to let the rope go with a buoy attached and the locals would come and dive for it later that day.

So Igor untied the anchor rope but with a gust of wind and a lurch from a swell he let go of the rope and the buoy rolled free over the side, both lost as he grabbed the rail. So he sailed back to Paihia for a third.

Igor's anchor bill was cheap compared to that of billionaire Ellison when he visited Auckland for the sailing of the 2002 America's Cup.

Ellison's boat *Oracle*, named after his software company, was involved in the racing and so he had his yacht *Katana* to use as his base for accommodation, race-watching and some sight-seeing.

He was in the Bay of Islands when a mate flew in from the US and landed at Auckland Airport. The friend was helicoptered to Mechanics Bay on the Auckland waterfront while Ellison and crew sped back down from Northland to pick him up. Then they refuelled.

I was reliably informed it cost $28,000 to top up

Katana's tanks. Then on the way back they hit some rougher headwinds and a bouncy chop, and one of the two forward anchors rumbled out of its casing. The rope chaffed and it fell overboard.

It went with a bang and the problem was identified immediately. The crew offered to drop a buoy and go back to get it. Ellison was in a hurry to make a dinner date at a Bay restaurant. He told them to forget it.

I wonder what that cost?

≈   ≈   ≈

THE *RIVA* SPEEDBOAT, named after the family of boatbuilders on Lake Iseo in northern Italy, is one of the finest–finished vessels ever made and to this day they still command the price for which they were sold, or far more — a rare achievement for anything that floats.

A few were built after World War One and by 1934, the *Riva*, driven by a four cylinder 1500cc inboard, had set a world water speed record of 80km/h.

A new model, the *Aquarama*, was launched into major production in 1962 with an American–built V8 motor capable of pushing the boat close to 100km/h. Boatbuilders made 3,760 of the sleek mahogany hull, leather lined boats between 1962 and 1996. Company owner Carlo Riva's office overlooked the production line.

He had the staff of different departments wear different coloured overalls, so when the red–coloured woodworkers and the yellow–coloured mechanics were deep in discussion he knew he had a problem.

Amongst the owners who gave the *Riva* fame were actors Richard Burton and Peter Sellers, Brigitte Bardot, Joan Collins and Sophia Loren. It was labelled the Rolls Royce of boats.

With their price at about $750,000, it soon became more popular to go for something bigger in fibreglass and plastic trim. The *Aquarama* remains a collector's item and always will be, while other boats deteriorate in value.

'It was just the sort of boat you'd expect a rock promoter to have – mirrored ceilings, jacuzzis, a leopard–skin everything. It made the vulgar seem commonplace.'
– Pamela Anderson in a line from her novel Star Struck.

The author

PETER JESSUP is a veteran journalist who has written about fishing and seafaring matters for more than 35 years. His work has appeared in many newspapers and magazines, including the *NZ Herald* and the *Auckland Star*.

He is the author of *Fishermen's Tales* and *The Complete History of New Zealand (in less than two hours)*, both published by Hurricane Press.

Jessup lives in Glen Eden, Auckland.